THE RICHEST COMEDIAN YOU'VE NEVER HEARD OF

Eric O'Shea

Copyright © 2020 Eric O'Shea
All rights reserved.

Book layout by ebooklaunch.com

To everyone who has ever believed in me—especially you, Ma!

Contents

INTRODUCTION 1

SO, YOU WANNA BE A STAND-UP COMEDIAN 3

INSPIRED IN A CHURCH HALL? BINGO! 7

GET OUT THERE, KID. YOU'RE ON! 10

ABANDON SHIP! 13

HAPPY NEW YEAR! 16

I'M READY FOR MY CLOSE-UP! 18

I HAD A GOOD "RUN" 21

FAME AND FORTUNE 26

'TIS THE SEASONING 30

SO WHAT IS THIS NACA THING ANYWAY? 33

WOW! YOU GET TO TRAVEL FOR A LIVING! 40

GOD DAMMIT, JUST DON'T SAY IT! 49

THE COLLEGE "CONTROVERSY" 51

SPEAK NOW OR FOREVER HOLD YOUR PEACE 61

THERE'S NO PLACE LIKE HOME 64

WHAM BAM, THANK YOU, SPAM 69

A DOSE OF REALITY . . . TV 75

WHERE HAVE YOU GONE, JOE DIMAGGIO? 89

DOCTOR! DOCTOR! GIVE ME THE VIEWS! 92

THE REVIEWS ARE IN! 95

FUN FACTS . . . ABOUT THE AUTHOR! 97

MY PET NAMED PEEVE 116

NYC AND ME	125
FEELING WEAK? YOUR DAILY MULTIVITAMIN	130
THE THREE THINGS FOR A REWARDING LIFE	132
SUNDAY SERMONS	136
CHILLS AND THRILLS!	140
UFO-HELL NO!	145
TOUCHED BY AN ANGEL	148
DR. E., RELATIONSHIP COUNSELOR	151
MY MANY LOVE AFFAIRS!	157
CHEW ON THIS	160
SO LONG, BUT NEVER GOODBYE	163
MY LIFE IN PICTURES	165

INTRODUCTION

Perfect! I got your attention with the title!

Well, I can assure you that it's not as arrogant as it sounds.

When you finally make it to the end of this book, I PROMISE that it will all come together and make perfect sense!

(Wow, why am I yelling?)

Because I am completely honored that you are here with me. For this is my first ever attempt to put any of my thoughts into a book. And again, I promise—no wait, I *guarantee*—that you will truly fall in love with it.

So please—please!—don't even think of stopping now.

The following chapters will be some of the most inspiring and thought-provoking messages you will ever read—and not just for comedy, but for life itself.

WARNING: No, this is not a how-to-do-comedy book, as there is no "right way" to do comedy. This also is not an autobiography. Yes, my life has been truly blessed, but I'll leave those kinds of books to the real heroes of the world. What follows are merely my opinions—opinions that I hope will spare you countless amounts of trial and error, frustration, and disappointment.

Right now, my goal is merely to get you thinking—and to (hopefully) inspire you.

I have a lot to say about comedy, particularly college comedy, and the world around us. And by sharing my experiences, I hope to support that simple but oh-so-important goal.

I want you to *thrive.*

I want you to *celebrate* your successes.

But I also want you to take a look yourself and consider where it is you want to go.

People are always saying we should "live in the moment." There's value in that, but it is just as important to envision who you *want* to be and to get excited about both of these existences. Your future—in both comedy and in life—is just as important as what you are experiencing right now.

Treat this dual journey with respect, for as a wise person once said, "May the eyes of the future look back upon you, and pray for you, that you may see beyond your own time."

This book is my journey. These are my stories. These are my thoughts.

Did I say that I'm honored you're here?

So honored.

Now let's dive in—together.

SO, YOU WANNA BE A STAND-UP COMEDIAN . . .

Let me ask you a question.

If you chose today, right now, to drop everything and become a stand-up comedian, where would you start?

Most people don't know.

Oh, I'm sure there'd be a few wise guys who would just smile confidently (because they are "the funny ones" at work) and say, "Well, I would probably just write some jokes. And, let me tell ya—I got some zingers, baby!"

Some might take a more "educational" route and pay for a class at some sort of comedy school, where they'd get some suggestions about how to hold the mic and how some words that start with *K* sound funny. After a few weeks, they'd then get their official certificate saying they passed the class, along with their five minutes to show off their "jokes" on stage for an evening.

But we are talking about making comedy a *career* here.

So, now what?

You don't know, do you?

Don't worry. Most people don't.

I didn't either.

Unlike the other 99 percent of career paths, there is no real preparation that will teach you how to do stand-up. There are no books to learn from. There is no formal college for it.

Sure, you can find extremely useful general information taught by some very qualified friends of mine (and some not so qualified), but when you look at the bigger picture of getting started, developing your act, making a name for yourself, earning a living, and keeping your sanity in one of the most brutal businesses out there (try to find me another that compares), I simply believe that a stand-up career cannot be taught, period.

And no, I am not tooting my own horn or being biased. Just think about it.

For one, it is just you. There is no real "help." You're not a part of some company. There is no team of workers to help pick up the slack and "get the job done."

There's just you—waking up every morning and mentally preparing for one hell of an unsure day.

Every day you'll be relying solely on your own *discipline* (the main reason why some very talented comics don't make it) to write material, to hit the phones, to sell yourself, and literally beg for stage time. Usually, unless the club owner likes your routine, it will be challenging to even get a spot. And even if you are liked, it's still not a sure thing. Often shows are already full because of the nineteen other new comics who beat you to it.

No, there are no guaranteed gigs in this business when you are starting out, so you keep emailing and calling until you get one. And even when you do get one and kill it up there, you are basically starting all over the very next day, hitting the phones and emails again for future spots. Nope, the club owners don't call you, and there is no inviting red carpet that magically leads you from your bedroom to the club stage.

But don't get upset by this. Even top club headliners have to do this every year to build their annual calendar. You just gotta be quick because booking stand-up gigs is usually first come, first served (not to mention the occasional rejection due to favorites and politics).

Most times, though, missing out on a gig has nothing to do with you, assuming you diligently tried to get it. It is merely a frustrating numbers game. Think about it. There are a kazillion comics out there and only fifty-two weeks in a year!

Consequently, there will be plenty of times when you are full of doubt.

One minute you're on stage destroying the room with people cheering and going absolutely nuts for you. The next minute you're in some cockroach-infested studio apartment, eating ketchup sandwiches and wondering how you're going to pay your rent and look relatively "financially desirable" enough to get a date. (And simultaneously pulling your hair out because if you don't find an ending to that one joke about tube socks, neither of those things will happen!)

But enough about my early years ...

When it comes to being a stand-up comedian, all I am saying is that you must be just as mentally strong as your physical effort in trying to book the gigs. There is no financial security in this business, and there is no guaranteed quality of life. So be prepared to watch other people take somewhat challenging but "safer" paths with great yearly salaries and strong personal relationships.

Again, in stand-up, there's just you, a notebook of scattered thoughts, and minimal stage time to even practice correctly. Often your audience will be intoxicated, miserable, or even more depressing, no one at all.

And on this journey through the unknown, you will encounter the bitter and the unethical—people you would normally never give the time of day to, but sadly have to put up with or proudly bypass—in order to advance your career.

How you move forward is up to you.

Yes, I've painted stand-up as very intimidating and daunting—and it is.

Most people cannot relate to even a *fraction* of what it takes to succeed in this business. Most people don't have to constantly reinvent a brand new way of doing their job. Most people are guaranteed that paycheck. So at times, you may internalize the stress and disappointment, culminating to that proverbial "breaking point" where you start to believe that taunting, condescending voice in your head. "Oh foolish one, why in the hell did you choose comedy as your career?"

But if this path is for you, you'll know deep down that you wouldn't change a thing.

Why?

Because you were *born* to do this, and you can't quit, no matter how hard you try.

Yes, you've chosen one of the most difficult, most scrutinized, most erratic careers and lifestyles that you could ever attach to your name and reputation.

And you wouldn't have it any other way.

So, don't you dare stop.

Just take a deep breath, give your heart a break, and get right back out there.

You're exactly where you need to be, and you're doing just great!

And if it helps, I'm always here for ya.

Always.

INSPIRED IN A CHURCH HALL? BINGO!

While most comics can trace their comedic inspiration back to a TV character or movie they watched as a kid, there is no question that my aha moment came from one very particular moment—and perhaps some divine intervention.

Now, channeling my best Sophia Petrillo from *Golden Girls* ...

Picture it. Hancock, New York. St. Paul's Church, 1977.

On a Wednesday at 7:30 p.m., my mom and her aunt Nell took me to play one of my favorite games, bingo, in a tiny farm town nestled on the Delaware River near the Pennsylvania border. It was simply a magical place for a vacation. It was right out of a fairy tale book. The country life—it just oozed utter and complete love.

It was so magical that our summer cottage on Crystal Lake, to my knowledge, didn't even have a zip code.

My grandpa George owned the Circle E Diner up there, right next to his house, and without a doubt, he was my male role model growing up. A simple but worldly man, he taught me how to drive, shave, work hard, and always maintain the highest moral character—sometimes quite sternly—but always with lots of humor and love.

From a seven-year-old-boy's perspective, my relatives from his huge family seemed to make up half the population of the area, as evidenced by the mammoth amount of food, tall tales, poker games, and laughter at our annual Labor Day family reunions.

The fun, traditions, and love were enough for a hundred lifetimes.

(Now, back to Sophia.) But I digress …

Anyway, I was taken to the church hall to play bingo.

While I sat in my metal folding chair, completely locked in to my one cardboard bingo card and just dying to win, I suddenly heard Joe Deserio, a.k.a., "the Man on the Mic."

I was simply captivated.

And I was no longer interested in winning. (OK, I still was. My Dallas Cowboys helmet-bank wasn't going to fill itself!)

But there I was, mesmerized by this magical man, Joe Deserio, welcoming us to the evening and starting the party for us regulars.

I couldn't take my eyes off him or focus on the game. There were moments that he'd either dramatically stall to say a number, or when a game was nearly over (*cue the scary music*), he'd very eerily say the final number, crushing everyone's hearts except for one lucky winner.

Other times he'd really crack us up by simply teasing the gal taking the bingo balls from him. With a sly smile, he'd pull each ball away, as if he just wasn't ready to let it go.

But whatever Joe did, it was incredible. You see, he was not only just calling out numbers.

He was *performing*.

And he owned that church hall, dammit! He owned everyone's attention. He owned the night. He was the man on center stage! (Well, technically to the left a bit and away from the kitchen, which was busy prepping boiled hot dogs and black coffee for intermission.)

But it was right then—right then—that I saw one man, for a long period of time, control a small crowd with just the sound of his voice, which echoed through a small metal instrument, that made him sound so much louder, and interestingly, so much more important, than anyone in the room.

Oh, I was hooked.

And had so many questions. How in the hell do you get to do what he's doing? Where in the hell do you go for such training? But for now, who cares. I simply *must* shake his hand.

And I got that chance. Soon after, when my grandpa and I were sitting in his diner booth on a quiet afternoon—wouldn't you know it?—in came the celebrity of Hancock, Joe Deserio, for a cup of coffee!

You have got to be kidding me! I thought.

I was starstruck. You would have thought that there was a limo outside. (Well, I don't know! Maybe he was on some kind of bingo tour.) I swallowed hard and had sweaty palms.

"You wanna talk to him?" Gramps asked with a smirk, just knowing how much I was dying to.

"Sure!" I said, smiling nervously yet excitedly.

"Hey, Joe!" Gramps said, with his signature chuckle. "Somebody wants to meet ya!"

"Of course!" Joe said with that Hollywood smile, spinning around on his round counter stool.

And right then—right then—after shaking his hand and sitting right next to him at the counter, I just knew that this was my calling. Well, maybe not bingo, but something.

But for now? It didn't matter.

Everything in the world was all right. I was the luckiest seven-year-old boy on the face of the planet—excited and simply enamored that I was rubbing elbows with the most famous man in town.

And who knows. As far as my newfound career was concerned, maybe Gramps could even be my manager.

Ah, yes. Sigh. A boy can dream.

GET OUT THERE, KID. YOU'RE ON!

September 16, 1993:

"And now, coming to the stage ... your final contestant of the evening! Not only is it his birthday, but it is his very first time performing—ever! So, how 'bout giving a warm welcome, everybody, for ... Eric O'Shea!"

None of the six people in the audience clapped, nor did the three "judges."

Yes, this is what I heard as I was standing outside of the Safe House—the local and legendary Milwaukee, Wisconsin, spy-themed bar and restaurant with secret passageways—waiting to come through the back door and directly on stage.

Moments earlier, I was pleading with the organizer to cancel my spot. Yep, serious anxiety. I could have just as easily crossed the street and walked home.

But this was an official comedy contest, featuring a whopping six comics, three judges, and five people in the crowd, all of them waiting to see who I was and what I could do.

It was too late to back out now. (Plus, as a man of the world, I figured my name on the sign-in sheet must have been a legally binding contract.)

This was it, the moment every broke, nervous, dressed-up-in-a-suit-and-tie, brand-new comic dreams of. After literally hours of rehearsing all day in a studio apartment, mimicking my grand entrance and five minutes of material, the time had come—the beginning of my comedy career!

As I walked on stage, and without even saying hello to the dozens of empty seats and one yawn, I accepted the light blinding my eyes and channeled my idol, Jerry Seinfeld, imitating his classic inflection in my opening line.

"Y'ever so tired in the morning that you start to put the cereal box back in the refrigerator?"

I stopped and just smiled. That's all I said, and I just waited for the crowd to crack up and blow the roof off its hinges after that *genius* observation.

Nothing. Crickets. No one moved.

I think I actually heard one lady blink.

I was in shock, frozen.

"What the hell? It worked for Jerry!" I heard my nervous inner voice whimper. "Oy, I knew I should have worn the *blue* tie."

No, it wasn't the tie.

And although things got a little better in the final four minutes—and by "better" I mean I think I saw someone mimic a smile and grimace as they adjusted their seat—I finished second to last in the contest. I guess one judge didn't want to ruin my birthday or felt bad that I moussed my hair for my big night.

But I did it. I actually did it. I followed through.

As I walked home by myself, my black dress shoes leading me up West Wisconsin Avenue for two miles, something just felt right.

So right.

I can't explain it or really put it into words, but if I had to, I would simply describe it as a very personal, unique experience—a magical experience—where you knew you'd just done something that you were born to do. That you actually wanted to do. That you *had* to do—again and again.

No, I'll never ever forget that reassured smile creeping up my face.

With my hands in my pockets, I replayed the night in my head.

That on my birthday, September 16, 1993, at twenty-three years of age, I walked onto a stage for the very first time to try stand-up comedy.

And that stage . . . felt like home.

ABANDON SHIP!

When you are a young, broke comic, you will take *any* damn gig you can get for stage time to practice, be heard, and pray for a laugh at the end of a joke.

Anywhere.

In front of anyone.

Well, kinda.

Two hell gigs, as they call them, come to mind that I still laugh about to this day. Wait—come to think of it, hell might be too nice of a place as the twenty-dollar pay and old turkey sandwich didn't even come close to dousing the flames.

The first one took place at a bowling alley.

When I showed up with my fifteen minutes of material (probably only two minutes of it was actually decent), the owner of the joint angrily told me, "Just stand there, don't touch anything, and sit tight," as he set up the microphone—*on lane five!*

With families bowling on each side of me in lanes four and six, I did my set.

I'm not quite sure what the most unfortunate part was: trying to be heard over the thunderstorm of balls and pins crashing together, or the two drunk guys way in the back of the bar playfully punching each other and yelling at me to "speak up, Slick!"

Needless to say, I threw my own gutter ball that night.

The second gig? An even worse setup. (And I use the term "setup" the same way I would describe my sex life as a twenty-four-year-old comic—nonexistent.)

You see, it took place at an old-folks home, where they told me to do thirty minutes in the middle of a gigantic ballroom. And I emphasize "middle," because there were about 150 very cute yet old, hard-of-hearing senior citizens, waaaay out in the distance—equally split up—on *both* sides of me.

That's right, seventy-five people on each side of me—waaaay far away to my left and waaaay far to my right—as I stared straight ahead at the brick wall directly in front of me.

So the next fifteen minutes, I had to turn to each side and yell each joke *twice* while getting stares and uncomfortable groans from both crowds.

Needless to say, it was then that I felt that horrible emotion that any new comic might feel when trying to entertain, not one, but two elderly audiences at the same time. That's right. I knew that I was bombing. Hard.

But then, out of nowhere—and don't ask me why—I made what some would say was a curious call. I made an executive decision to ditch every last bit of audible material I had, reach into my nearly empty bag of tricks, and do what any young, hopeless comic might do. I desperately reached out my hand toward the only old person who was smiling and barely focusing on me, carefully helped him up, and began to slow dance with him.

It was a hit.

We twirled and dipped our way for the next fifteen minutes as I hummed songs in the mic and sang to my new dance partner—better known now as my saving grace.

How I got through it or why the crowd loved it, I'll never know. But they all hooted and hollered, clapped and cheered as if they just saw the most original, top-notch vaudeville act. Some actually raised their hands to dance with me next!

To be honest, I don't remember too much about what happened that night, and quite frankly, I'm not quite sure if I want to. But I do remember being thankful that I had a gig—any gig—and that I survived.

Because with my dancing done, as I said good night (and ready to never show my face in South Milwaukee again) I couldn't believe what happened next.

The crowd oddly cheered for more.

"Encore! Encore" I heard.

Thankfully, from both sides.

HAPPY NEW YEAR!

Working New Year's Eve as a comic is always a little more special and prestigious than other gigs. To be chosen by a club owner, out of all the other comics around, to ring in the new year with the staff and audience, that's something special.

Well, unless you're me—the emcee.

December 31, 1993: Only three months into my comedy journey, the owner of the club where I started in Milwaukee told me I could emcee the New Year's Eve festivities at a sister club in Madison, Wisconsin.

Are you kidding me? It was like being called up to play in the major leagues!

So, with a fifty-dollar bill in my pocket—the only money to my name from the past week's pay—and dressed in my only snazzy suit for the weekend (I wanted to be stage ready in case of a delay), I headed out on a Greyhound bus, in a snowstorm, with the temperature outside a balmy negative nineteen degrees.

And for some extra anxiety? I was also heading into my own personal lion's den, as the blunt, moody club owner had previously banned one of my jokes because, in his words, "It sucks and is absolutely awful!"

So, I had to do well.

Oh, the joke? OK, I'll tell ya, if you can handle me trying to channel my inner Jerry Seinfeld again.

Y'ever notice at a fancy holiday house party, there's always that one room where people put their coats? Y'ever think, Hmm ... maybe the coats are having a party of their own? Maybe they are all intertwined on the bed, dancing, and twirling each other with their sleeves. And at the end of the night? You just *know* the two guy coats call up each other very slyly and say, "So, Steve ... did you get in her pockets?"

Yep. Banned. He said I would never work his club if I did that joke, ever.

So, I didn't. I was home free.

Well, that is until I then found myself hotel-less for the night.

(Again, it's New Year's Eve, I'm in my suit, and every hotel is sold out.)

The club owner then confessed, "I didn't book you a room. You'll stay at my house." And with it being too late to take a bus home and the temperature negative nineteen degrees, I didn't have much of a choice.

So, in a very modest ranch-style house, on the couch, in my suit, and with just the glow of the TV flickering in the living room, I tried my best to get a good night's sleep. Emphasis on "tried."

Why? Well, let's just say that he and a gal pal from the waitstaff were having their own loud, ahem, "after-party" doin' the ol' Posturepedic dosey doe in one of the back bedrooms.

So . . . what did this emcee, on the bottom of the comedic totem pole do? Well, too nervous to say or do anything (remember, he already hated my coat joke), and with my head on a hard, square couch pillow, I found myself suddenly thanking God for discovering the only thing that could give me some peace and quiet: the TV remote's volume button.

Yes, it was turned up quite high—I think as far as it could go—drowning out the noise from the "other show" that was airing.

Ah, yes, the good ol' volume button.

The best New Year's Eve date I've ever had.

I'M READY FOR MY CLOSE-UP!

MODELS WANTED! (Bring Photo)

This was the ad that I saw one hot day in the *New Haven Register* in the summer of 1991.

But did I fit the criteria? That was a trick question.

Of course I did!

I knew I had boy-band good looks—and I'm not just talkin' about any ol' boy-band good looks. I'm talkin' 'bout New Kids on the Block good looks. Don't believe me? Hell, here's my ace in the hole: my mom. She *always* told me how handsome I was.

So, check and check!

I mean, what else does one need to become a famous model? These people wanted the next Ralph Macchio? They were going to get the next Ralph Macchio.

But hmm . . . what kind of picture should I take? I knew my photo had to "speak to the people," but it also had to sell merchandise. It couldn't just be all about me, usually a very hard concept for a young model to understand. And I needed to look powerful, yet not too over the top.

But most of all, it had to be subtle. Too many young models make the mistake of professionally posing in a warehouse or on some abandoned train tracks with their hair blowing in the breeze.

But nope, not this guy . . .

So with my tight gold chain and my hair channeling John Turturro, I went with a nature shot of me holding my bichon frise dog, Sammy, while gazing into the distance from behind my front screen door.

And I don't mean to brag, but, yes, it only took one shot to capture the magic.

I was a natural.

So after writing my name, address, landline phone number, and suit and shoe size on the back of my picture, I was now ready to go to the address from the ad and launch a career. Arriving deep in some tiny, woodsy town in rural Connecticut, I found the office building with the address out in front. And after giving myself a quick once-over and a cool wink in the rearview mirror of my cherry-red Chevy Nova, I strutted in with my photo hot off the press. If there was a waiting room full of wannabes, they could just take their butts home, because the real deal was about to walk in.

"Can I help you?" asked the receptionist.

Smooth and in my best model voice, I replied, "Mm ... yes. I'm here for the modeling?"

"Do you have a headshot?"

Not knowing what a headshot was, I played it off. "No, but I have *this*," I said, whipping out my bichon pic, "and, um, I'm a-gonna need it back, because it's the only copy I have, but here," I said with a cocked eyebrow and a model pout. "Take a look."

After five seconds of silence—clearly because she was blown away by the fresh, new look they were going for—the lady looked puzzled and said, "Um, OK. Well, I'll jot down your phone number here, and ... um ... weeee will get in contact with you." (She had a great forced smile.)

"Well, all right," I said, still smiling and confident. "And again, I'm a-gonna need that photo back." (*Wink*.)

"Oh yes. Of course, of course!" she quickly said. "You don't want to lose your only copy!"

I took back the photo with just the tips of my index and middle fingers, mumbling under my breath. "Yep, always leave them wanting more."

But then I went for the kill and closed the deal with this final parting shot. "Oh, and just so you know, my schedule is pretty wide open all this week. Dairy Queen has me workin' nights." (wink goodbye)

I then drove home knowing I'd just hit it out of the park. I'd perfectly demonstrated how a young boy could use his God-given talents and razor-sharp instincts. "Get ready for greatness, my friend!" I screamed in the summer wind with all the car windows down. "Oh, and no one—NO ONE—better be using the landline when I walk in the door either!" (I had to be ready just in case they needed me to fill in for a sudden cancellation.)

They didn't call that day.

And twenty-five years later, I'm still waiting.

Hmm, I wonder what it was?

Maybe I should have just given them the photo to keep? Maybe there was some kind of jealousy going on behind the scenes? (We all know how insecure the people in this business can be.)

Oh, wait a minute. I know what it was!

(And I'm saving the dramatic picture reveal for the end of this book!)

It's so obvious.

Yep, that's right.

I just simply had a look, "ahead of my time."

I HAD A GOOD "RUN"

When you've put in as many years and shows as I have, you learn there's no such thing as just traveler's diarrhea.

There's only trying-not-to-shit-your-pants-in-front-of-hundreds-of-people.

So . . . without any further ado . . . as I now pay tribute to and echo the dramatic intro of *Law and Order*, these are my stories.

SHUNG! SHUNG!

The setting: Salve Regina University, which ironically is Latin for "an explosion of the Fruit of the Looma."

So there I was, at one of the most beautiful campuses I have ever seen—literally castle-like buildings gorgeously nestled by the Atlantic Ocean. It's something right out of those Blue Mountain greeting cards. I was absolutely starving and running on only a few hours of sleep. With an already bad history with dairy, I wisely decided to scarf down five gigantic, greasy, gooey mozzarella sticks. Yes, you could actually see the thick, melted cheese chunks stretching out and getting lodged in my throat, requiring a huge effort to completely swallow.

Then, after using practically a whole roll of paper towels to wipe my hands and feeling a ten-pound block of hot, thick goo plunging down to my stomach—ta-da! It was showtime! (*Jazz hands!*)

Now you know how you just don't forget some things, like how something is so memorable, that you can recount *every* detail?

Well, there I was with over three hundred students in front of me, and the show could not have been going any better. Then, exactly thirty-three minutes into my set, I had just finished a joke about counting money, when the scariest, loudest rumble of pressure along the front-left side of my beltline buckled me over in pain.

I literally couldn't move. It was like a knife stabbing right into my pelvis. And although I smiled and took a deep breath as the sweat formed on my upper brow, I just knew that this was not good. I knew I was in deep, deep trouble.

So, what did I do for the last twenty-seven minutes of my show?

Well, you know how UFO abductees have claimed to have "lost time" where they have no memory of anything?

All I remember was sitting down on an old, hard steel stool, clenching my sphincter muscle and butt cheeks together as tightly as I could, sweating and shaking while trying to avoid an explosion that would— how can I put this?—perhaps cause the university to go on total lockdown.

Yes, campus police and all.

Then, out of nowhere—don't ask me how— but I then vaguely remember hearing the final song to my closing bit.

No way. You're kidding me? I made it?

Kinda. Now for my much-needed emergency escape route to Anywhere-but-heresville.

So, after screaming good night, still sweating and shaking and completely out of any anus control, I raced to the bathroom behind me, leaving the emcee and three hundred people wondering why I had jumped off the back of the five-foot makeshift stage and into an old men's room.

Fast-forward twenty minutes . . . the crowd had already left, and four student activities members were sitting quietly, just waiting for me in an empty, echoey auditorium. I emerged pale and exhausted and told them (wait for it) that I ran to the bathroom because I was just so super excited to put on the school sweatshirt that they gave me before the show!

I wasn't even wearing the sweatshirt.

They knew. Everybody knew. And it was one of the most awkward rides back to the hotel.

But wait. The fun doesn't end there.

(*Cue the cheesy game-show host yelling.*) SSSSpeaking of rides back to the hotel, how about the time I sat in a seat previously occupied by someone who, unfortunately, must have had some sort of, um, incontinence problem? (Poor thing, but …)

Yep, that's right.

As I got back to my room, and feeling a little odd, I noticed the strongest smell of fresh, warm, dark-yellow urine that had created a *giant* wet spot on my entire behind. It was so bad that my jeans and underwear were literally stuck to my cheeks. I literally had to pinch-peel them off and toss them out. (Oh, and because I am such a wimp with bodily fluids—especially bodily fluids that, ya know, *aren't mine*—I dry heaved while doing it the whole time … just for the record)

But without a doubt, the story that *unequivocally tops it all,* was when I had just finished a noon show in ninety-five-percent humidity and, for some reason, decided to chug down a family-sized bowl of creamy lobster bisque on an empty stomach.

I now want you to fast-forward to the same sweating, shakes, pressure, and an exhausted sphincter muscle trying to hold in the pain of exploding as before.

But this time?

I'm in a rental car, stuck in traffic, inside the Lincoln Tunnel …

Trapped in a complete dead stop …

With nowhere to go . . .

So with me gripping the steering wheel as tightly as I could, bent over, trying to butt-swallow that barely leaking pressure of hot mess, as I endeavor to buy another ten seconds of precious time. I frantically undid my seat belt, pulled down my pants, and placed the driver's-side floor mat underneath my butt. I was trying to protect the car here. After all, it was a rental, and let's be honest. If there was a hundred-dollar smoking fine, imagine the cost (financially, emotionally, and spiritually) of shitting all over the front seat.

Then, to make it worse—you just knew it had to get worse—there was a tractor trailer behind me, whose driver could *absolutely* see downward through my back windshield and watch the whole thing.

But you know what? Who cares. I had bigger problems.

But just then, the traffic starts to move along, and I literally see the "light at the end of the tunnel."

Then, I'm out of the tunnel!

And with every ounce of strength I have left in my butt muscles, I zip over to the curb of 41st street, jump out of the car with my pants undone—and still trembling—do the only classy, respectful move I could think of: squat over a potted plant right outside someone's giant ground-floor terrace window *in broad daylight.*

And yes, they were home. Yes, there were dozens of people on their lunch hour walking mere inches above my head. And no, me tucking my chin down to my chest didn't make me any more invisible.

But I still had to wipe. So with nothing to use and more eyes on me than I care to imagine, I removed my T-shirt, "used" it, tossed it atop the potted plant, and ran out of there with that tiny bit of dignity I had left. And that was that.

But ladies and gentlemen?

(*Long, dramatic pause.*)

THE RICHEST COMEDIAN YOU'VE NEVER HEARD OF

It was over.

And just like the final scene of a war movie, when the smoke clears after a bombing, and all you see is the massive devastation and very few survivors, all I heard was the sound of that helicopter coming to get me.

Bare chested, on my knees, and my arms exhaustedly stretched out to the sky, I survived that fateful day, my friends.

So, when you see me, don't forget to thank a veteran.

May God bless you, and may God bless us all.

(*Quick salute.*)

FAME AND FORTUNE

I won't lie. At my graduation from Marquette University in 1992, a very wide-eyed and naive Young Eric wrote out the title of this chapter in masking tape on top of his cap for everyone to see. To be honest, if I was able to fit "marrying a supermodel" as well, I probably would have had that on there too. At the time, fame and fortune exemplified success and swagger for me. But little did I know that in a career such as comedy, which has so many variables and constantly requires self-discovery, those two words would eventually take on a whole different meaning.

But before we go on, I want to be clear and honest about something. This chapter is not about trying to justify my career or me being a sour grape, for it is actually quite the opposite. And I especially want young comics (and young anybody) to know this. Although you may not have society's definition of fame and fortune, you can still have it *all*—all that you desire in life, all on your terms, all with authenticity, positive energy, and pure joy.

And as corny as that sounds (and I know it does), I'd be honored to be that example for you here. This chapter is a teaching moment, and the lesson is to learn thankfulness.

Allow me to explain.

There is no question that when you are young, excited, and starting out in anything, you forecast this huge vision of what your life will look like—and usually fame and fortune are somewhere at the forefront. But other factors you don't account for—things like sacrifice, comfort, priorities, happiness, and contentment—eventually appear out of nowhere, and turn out to be so much more important than anything you could ever envision.

I have always told young comics that the business we chose is one with no proverbial ceiling. You can be as big and rich as your talent takes you. And unlike how most careers that "cap off" at a certain point, there is really no stopping your ascension in comedy to an iconic, legendary status. But as the years go by, and you realize the full complexity of the situation, you organically begin to take stock in other undeniable variables that have been around forever—things like time, energy, love, family, and values.

And at the end of the day, these are the only variables that truly matter.

Now, again, I am not trying to discourage anyone here or paint with a broad brush to say that you can't have it all. Of course you can, and some people have done so wonderfully with talent, class, and grace.

But in doing so, there comes an even more important question as your career ascends: Do you even want to have it all? I know that sounds like a crazy question, but for me, after having experienced a few Hollywood moments and having grown as a person, I realized that it was essential for me, and what I believed in, to take some essential detours to where I wanted to go.

I saw firsthand the tremendous amount of sacrifice that fame and fortune demanded of my values, energy, and time. I also didn't see any payoff whatsoever from being a public figure stuck in the spotlight, with little to no privacy, and being scrutinized about everything from your hair to your bank account.

I mean, what kind of life is that? To be blunt, I don't see that lifestyle as very comfortable or even healthy. And if you don't believe me, just look at the swarm of paparazzi blocking a celebrity's path—as they literally try to grieve walking to a funeral!

Um, no. That's *not* for me. I value my privacy and dignity way too much for that kind of existence.

And again, is it always like that? And aren't there some "satisfying" financial perks to being famous? I suppose. But to be honest—and I've genuinely laughed about this to myself—I would have zero idea about what to do with all that money. Now, yes, I hear the critics screaming, "What? Hell, give it to me! I'll take it! I'd know what to do with it!"

OK, I'm sure there are some fun things to do with a lot of money, but when you look at your life right now—and I mean *really* look at it with 100 percent honesty—are you really "doing without"? I mean, how many cars, clothes, and expensive dinners does one need?

Now, some guys try to stump me with a cocky tone. "OK, Eric. Riiight, so you wouldn't want to have a Porsche sitting outside and some gourmet chef preparing all the food you can eat?"

And every time, I've calmly but incredulously raised my voice, "No! Why? So I could shit my pants in the front seat of my Porsche from overeating? Did you not read the chapter on my sensitive stomach in the Lincoln Tunnel, you whore?!"

Fine, I don't call them whores, but we always share a good laugh when naysayers realize my point: money gives you options—many options—but it does not make you happy. No matter how much money you have, you are still you—with all your bodily flaws, mental hang-ups, and ridiculous habits. (Heck, I love naps so much, I'd probably sleep all my money and fame away!)

The point is, fame and fortune come with a cost and, to me, really don't change the core of who you are. Instead, you have to make huge sacrifices, take on lots of unnecessary stress, and in most cases, lose some of your individuality—the one thing that nothing should ever take away from you.

And think about it. With all the Hollywood scandals, temptations, immorality, and huge loss of self that comes from living in a fan-based world that only shows the "good times" and the "final product"—in a world that requires immense sacrifices and leads to the downward spirals of so many celebrities attempting to please total strangers that, in a weird way, both crave living vicariously through celebrities and actually enjoy the front-page headlines of Hollywood instability—you must ask yourself, Is fame and fortune really worth it?

With the utmost respect for everyone's personal choices and journey, I personally don't think so.

And sorry to keep repeating myself, but I have to say it again—not with arrogance or to protect my ego, but because I am so honored to have learned so much about myself over the years—I simply could not have asked for a better life.

Now, are there still some projects that I'm excited to pursue and some growth that I'd like to have as a human being? Of course. But I thank God every day for being so very good to me.

So as you make your journey, I simply ask that you take into account what you really want out of comedy and your life.

But as for me, Mr. Minimalist, my faith, health, family, a few bucks in my pocket, some admirers, and the pure joy of life is way more than enough for this guy.

Oh, and my Imodium too …

Please stop smiling.

I said *stop*!

'TIS THE SEASONING

Dear New Comics,

I am sure that you have all heard the old saying, "Variety is the spice of life." Well, not so fast. As a matter of fact, please go right now to your mental spice rack and *toss it out*.

Don't get me wrong. Variety is wonderful when it comes to things like foods, vacations, and dating. You simply have to find out what you like and how you like it. And yes, without a doubt, it is truly satisfying when you capture that part of your identity.

But I will say this. When you are starting out in comedy and pursuing the college market, any variety in how you approach comedy might not be your best friend. Well, at least for now.

I often get asked, "What is the most important thing you need to be successful in the college market?" My answer has never wavered. It takes discipline.

Consistent, unwavering discipline.

That's right. Good ol' Aristotle was definitely on to something when he said, "Excellence is not a singular act, but a habit. You are what you repeatedly do."

And I try to live up to that mantra every day and in everything I do. Believe me, it isn't easy—especially when we are all faced with the challenges of our own unique combination of genetics and environment.

Yes, we all have our own stories.

THE RICHEST COMEDIAN YOU'VE NEVER HEARD OF

For me, it was being a slightly OCD, observant but apprehensive, self-appointed mama's boy whose parents divorced when he was twelve. Mom had three jobs and once only made $11,000 in a year for four people to live on. There were also some very lean stretches regarding food and heat (cereal and pasta was cheap and very easy to make while huddling upstairs because it was freezing downstairs).

Outside the house? Well, not to sound like a Bill Cosby skit, but sometimes I *did* walk to school by myself at six in the morning, while it was still dark out, in the snow, and for about two miles—just to serve mass as an altar boy before school. As for my employment, well, it was whatever provided a paycheck. Throughout the years, I found myself holding the random, esteemed titles of camp counselor, Dairy Queen server, and—wait for it—hospital security guard. That last one really didn't go well because doctors really can't have the security guard passing out at the sight of blood while trying to handcuff a drunk who split his head open. (Yeah, I'm pretty sure he didn't respect my badge. Well, actually no one did.)

Yes, I was forced to grow up fast, but all the while I maintained focus and *discipline*. (And there's that word again.)

So what does "discipline" really mean?

Well, first of all, it varies from person to person—as, again, we all have our own set of circumstances. However, I do believe that there is one common denominator: creating healthy habits that you adhere to without fail every day.

You see, when I started comedy, I was broke, like many other new comics. I literally ate ketchup sandwiches for months because I needed to pay rent and have gas money to get to my emcee gigs. (Although, this is probably a bad example of sacrifice because I still love a bottle of ketchup or BBQ sauce with a loaf of bread!)

But back to the violin music.

On occasion, I'd also sleep in my 1989 Ford Escort to save a few bucks. And no, those Milwaukee winters were not fun. Do you know that I once actually pumped only $3.83 of my $5.00 because the frigid wind in negative forty-nine-degree weather was whipping down my lungs so bad I literally couldn't breathe?!

I just left.

But I knew that this is what I had to do to give myself a chance at being successful. I just had to dedicate my life to consistently focusing on my goals, where splurging, partying, or "treating myself" seemed counterproductive.

I lived this way daily, with no days off, and without fail. (Although, having never taken a puff of anything in my life, getting tipsy on only one glass of pinot grigio, and having my senior prom as my very first date, I wasn't exactly giving up life in the fast lane.)

But back to you, the young comic.

What I'm simply trying to say is this: in comedy, specifically the college market, I found out that being around a very long time requires that same type of discipline, just applied to how you prepare and perform for a school.

These gigs entail way more than just "doing a show." Actually, you probably wouldn't believe the amount of detail it involves.

So get a drink, grab a snack, hunker down, and get ready for me to tell you a little about the world of (*fancy drum roll*) . . . NACA!

(*Cymbal crash.*)

Wow, did you feel that? Exciting stuff, right?

(*Quickly wiggles eyebrows up and down while smiling.*)

Oh, sorry. Next chapter.

SO WHAT IS THIS NACA THING ANYWAY?

NACA is the National Association for Campus Activities.

It is one of the most unique, amazing, rewarding, profitable, relationship- building, challenging, tricky, constantly evolving, classy, comfortable, loose, professional, fun, thought-provoking, steeped-in-tradition, organized, exhausting, thrilling, and seemingly timeless market you could ever be a part of in both stand-up comedy and performing—to put it vaguely (*wink*).

Now let me walk you through the most common way to get involved, though there are certainly many paths.

Let's begin. You are a stand-up comedian who would just love to work in a market with the wonderful attributes listed above. (Why would you *not* want to?) But to do that, you have to be ready, and that pretty much means having an hour of clean, relatable, uncontroversial content for students between the ages of eighteen and twenty-one.

Got that? Great.

Now you—or even better, and agent with connections and a reputation—need to submit a three-minute sample of your best material. No, that was not a typo. You only get *three minutes* to impress them. Who is "them"? A committee of advisors, staff, and experienced board members who watch your three minutes and determine if you are both funny and the right fit for the conference.

So yes, they only watch three minutes—and not even all at once!

Oh, and did I say getting into NACA is competitive? Yep. There are between three hundred and four hundred acts vying for only about forty-five highly coveted spots to perform for the conference weekend.

And it gets even tougher.

Because there are so many submissions, the judging is broken down into three separate rounds. That's right. Three rounds of judging from that three-minute clip of yourself. So say there are five hundred submission clips. After the first round of watching (and note this) from only *one minute* of each submission clip, there are now two piles that are created—a moving-on-to-the-next-round pile and a no pile.

The no pile doesn't move on, but the yes pile endures two more rounds of viewing, each involving the next minute of each clip.

By narrowing the field little by little, the judges eventually come up with the highly coveted forty-five acts for the conference weekend.

What and where is this conference?

NACA divides the entire United States into regions, and then schools from those regions come to a fancy hotel conference center within their region to watch those forty-five acts perform. Usually the school is represented by a staff advisor and anywhere from two to ten students who are learning how to book acts while enjoying a fun weekend with some great entertainment.

There is also a national convention where any school can attend from any region, and try not to get lost because this is the really big one where there's lots of variety, competition, and excitement.

O.K. You just got selected! Congratulations! Now what?

After paying a small fee to NACA, you and your agent then get notified about which of the three days and times you will be performing in the three-day conference. There are day spots and highly coveted night spots. Naturally, opening night is great with the energy, excitement, and anticipation of the crowd. The second night is also terrific as people have had a chance to settle in and evaluate the first night. The third and final day? It's still an honor to perform. Yes, people are tired after having seen so many showcases as part of a *nonstop* schedule (you have no idea!) but you still have plenty of opportunity to get bookings.

Whether you perform in a daytime slot or a nighttime slot is randomly determined and up to NACA's discretion. Yes, some spots can then be more advantageous than others, but guess what? Even if you get the very last day and perform for a sleepy afternoon crowd whose energy and school budgets are dwindling, you still treat it with respect. Act like you belong and don't change your approach.

Think about it. The hundreds of acts that didn't make the cut would absolutely kill for that spot!

So how much time do you get to perform?

Well, an emcee spot gets twenty-five minutes. And I've enjoyed that spot for many years, but it's not easy. Not only are you the host of the showcase, but your act is broken down into five smaller sets! Yep, you are steering the ship, and that entails the very tricky juggling act of not only selling your jokes and introducing acts, but going right back out there—right after a musical act, comic, or serious slam poet might have quickly changed the entire mood of the room for "the worse."

It is your job to be quick, funny, and grab them right back, both for the audience's enjoyment and for the sake of your bookings.

But don't worry. Most acts that start at NACA do the straight, shorter, fifteen-minute set where you just get in, get out, and keep your flow. This is a lot easier.

OK, great job! You just finished, and all six acts in your showcase finished too. So now what?

Well, after the showcase is over, it is time for the marketplace!

This is go time.

The marketplace is a gigantic area made of agency booths where, after your set, you show your credentials at the door and find your booth. Your agent will have your credentials all set up and waiting for you, or you will simply go over to the booth together. At your agency booth will be all your promo materials (T-shirts, giveaways, your calendar, etc.), and this where you do your business, build relationships, and get immediate feedback on your set.

And you will.

Because when that NACA staff member yells in the mic, "The marketplace is now open," all of those students that just watched you kill at your showcase literally come running in like wildfire, desperately trying to find you and other acts that did really well. They will want to talk to you, shake your hand, take pictures, and most of all, book you for the academic year at their campus. Now, the marketplace has a set time (and there are only a few throughout the conference weekend), so make sure to really be "on": friendly, energetic, professional, and tactful. Really take in the moment. The students will be so excited to see you, it'll feel like Christmas morning!

So now you got some good leads, solid bookings, and interest. Now what?

After the showcasing is done and the marketplaces have concluded comes perhaps the most important part for both you, your agent, and your living.

The block booking room.

This is the room where all the magic takes place, and although it is not mandatory, the schools are encouraged to attend to solidify any interest in your show.

The block booking room serves two purposes: (1) to keep interest focused on schools within a certain geographical area so you don't have to travel crazy routes, and (2) to then give those schools a discount for being so flexible and considerate for keeping you in a certain area.

Now let me back up a bit. (Sorry, I'm excited explaining this.)

In the conference program for the weekend, there is your headshot, bio, and three lists of pricing. The first price is called your *isolated price*, and this is the price for a school to just have you for one night—hence "isolated"—and it is the most expensive price.

The next tier, is what is called the *three-of-five block*. Remember how I said the schools are encouraged to keep you in an area and then are rewarded with a discount? Well, if three schools join a block (it is called the block booking room, after all), then those schools will get that lower three-of-five price. Plus, you'll have great routing. The third tier is called the *five-of-seven block* and follows the same concept. If at least five schools near each other want to keep you in a certain area, they will all get an even lower price—and guess what? You are now being booked quite a lot in one area too!

It's a win-win for everyone.

Oh, and keep in mind, with all our modern-day devices, block booking can even be done at either the conference or online back at campus. This flexibility is great since schools sometimes do not want to book right away, preferring to process the exciting weekend a bit more and make a decision later about who they want to bring to campus.

But don't worry. If you've made a great impression, they won't forget about you.

Well, don't look now, but congratulations! You've now got a tour!

But, phew—it is quite a process, isn't it?

I'm telling you, this is not like a club, cruise ship, or corporate show where you might simply be "recommended" by someone or have the advantage of sending in a longer demo of jokes—including jokes that have, ahem, much more leeway to actually be said on stage.

Nope. With NACA, again, you get three minutes to impress the selection committee enough to choose you over hundreds of other acts—after three rounds of judging. Then you have to kill at the convention—including during marketplace and block booking sessions—to stand out and get bookings.

And you have to do all of this with class, energy, professionalism, and optimism.

The process is daunting, but my advice is this. Do not be nervous, and just enjoy the process. Just do what you do best, but be ready to be flexible—on both material and scheduling. Do not stop observing and learning. Take everything in, measuring responses to your set list and the energy the crowd gives each day.

But most importantly, ask lots of questions. Ask about everything. Agents and veteran acts could not shut me up, as I was soooo eager to find the right formula both on and off the stage.

And I wasn't being dramatic earlier. There are no breaks in the weekend schedule for the schools and students. They are always attending something!

Bouncing between showcases, dinners, marketplaces, and bookings from sunrise to sundown, college reps will be up at the crack of dawn and not go to bed till after midnight. It is a three-day adrenaline fest like nothing you have ever experienced.

So just be prepared as you only get one real opportunity to make a killer impression. And whatever you do, just stay positive! This is a business, and it takes some time to settle into the market.

But most of all—and I wanna punch myself in the face right now because I hate this expression when something is new and a little daunting—have fun!

This is supposed to be *fun*!

Don't think of the results. Don't think of the other acts. Don't think of expectations. Don't think of anything else other than having fun on that stage and just doing your best.

There is a specific rhythm to this college market, and it takes time to feel it. But you will find it, and you will fit in just fine.

And I promise you, if you come prepared, enjoy yourself, take it all in, and make adjustments as necessary, you will be this much closer to what could be decades of not only enjoying a fantastic career doing what you love, but more importantly, building some incredible relationships.

So get excited, and always remember that it is a great honor to be in this market.

And if you treat it with love . . .

It will love you right back.

WOW! YOU GET TO TRAVEL FOR A LIVING!

Congratulations! You just booked a gazillion dates at NACA and are super thankful!

And I can't stress that last point enough. I am always grateful for being chosen to perform. I mean, think about it. Your creativity and hard work just got you invited to be a part of a very selective campus programming calendar!

Now there is only one thing keeping you from the all the fun, laughs, and memories: the darn distance to the schools!

Well, buckle up, my friend, because as my great-great-grandmother Ida used to say back in the 1880s, "It's about to get motha-effin' REAL up in here!"

You see, whereas most people do their little, annoying twenty-minute commute to work every day and complain about that damn traffic light that takes too long on State Street, try this on for size.

(And you might actually wanna grab something to drink for this part.)

It's 4:00 a.m. You're on your eighth city in nine days, already mentally and physically exhausted from all the travel, not to mention all the work you've done with your show material. You're on four hours of sleep, and because it was a late show, you simply have to be up this early to give yourself enough drive time to get back to the airport.

It's also the dead of winter and freezing outside.

THE RICHEST COMEDIAN YOU'VE NEVER HEARD OF

You're in your first (and notice I said "first") rental car of the day for about a ninety-minute drive with your GPS on. You finally make it and now have to refill the tank outside a gas station. No one is around, not a soul. You are now extra freezing and staring at a ghost town, and as the tank is filling, you stand there with the wind whipping across your face. You're bundled up, thankfully, but still you ruminate about the rest of your insane week of travel and the shows to come.

You return the car, the keys, and quickly walk (in the cold) with your luggage into the warm comfort of the airport—only to fight long security lines, wait at the gate, and pray for no maintenance delay, crew problem, or sudden cancellation.

The snow is starting to fall, but no delays. Wow, you got lucky!

Damn. Spoke too soon.

You're now on the plane, but they have to de-ice the wings.

"Oh my gosh, it's already been twenty-six minutes! Will I make my connection?"

Your heart beats faster. An entire crowd was excited at NACA, and now your whole reputation, livelihood, and paycheck are waiting for you in the next city!

You call the school to tell them the situation, trying to stay chipper and positive but hoping you won't have to sleep on the floor and wait for a new flight.

And then it's announced throughout the cabin. Due to the de-icing delay, your plane is now number seventeen for take-off. Reality hits you. You will not make your connection.

Let me tell you, it's hard to feel so helpless with so much on the line.

You take a sip of water trying to gather yourself. You wish you had an assistant, a secretary—anyone to help. But it's just you.

So you first call Avis to change your second car reservation of the day to match your new arrival time. You finally get to your connection city, and after sitting on a two-hour flight, landing at the second airport, and running top speed to the gate, you barely—just barely—make that puddle-jumper flight to your final destination, out of breath but thankful.

But you're not even close to being done yet.

You land, get in that second rental car, drive another ninety minutes to the town where the show is, fighting local traffic along the way. Remember those traffic jams nine-to-fivers talk about?

Yeah, you just hit that now too.

Exhausted, you then finally find the hotel, get out of the car, and wait at the front desk. There is now a problem with your room because a busload of high schoolers was in town for a big game the night before. The clerk then, with a smile, calmly asks you to hold as he answers the phone. You finally get your room key after signing some exhausted version of your signature on the registration form and are dying to lie down on a bed—even for just two minutes—before you have to perform and be on for two hundred excited, screaming students.

You walk to the other end of the hotel. Why the hotel clerk put you on the top level by the back entrance, you have no freakin' idea. And now the room key doesn't work, so you go back downstairs, then back to your room, and finally text the school that you made it. (And I use the phrase "made it" rather loosely.) You arrange a pickup time in the lobby, showering quickly, and, oh yeah, go over that one new joke you hope works out in your set.

After all, it's one of the only things that really matter in this business: the jokes and the show.

Sorry to say it, but what just happened in your travel day has nothing to do with the crowd, their excitement, and the performance—you know, the main reason why you made this long journey!

And now it's showtime.

THE RICHEST COMEDIAN YOU'VE NEVER HEARD OF

It's just you in front of all those psyched students, not to mention the activity members and adviser who graciously hired you at NACA. They all want your performance to be top notch—engaging, hilarious, and worth the trip from their residence halls.

Don't get me wrong about your long journey. I certainly can relate to a long travel day. But the bottom line—and I'm gonna be blunt—is this: with all the excitement in the theater, those people couldn't care less about your travel day from hell. And that is not a criticism of anyone at the school. It is just reality.

Their minds are, and rightly so, focused on the show.

Keep in mind that the school also put in tons of work to make this date and show come together. There's reserving the auditorium, tons of promotion, staffing, meetings, audio and tech to help with sound check …

Bottom line? You simply have to respect their effort too.

So anyway, back to the show.

Now get excited, because a student is about to introduce you. And boom! You're on!

And not to frighten any young comics, but let's now talk about all that "you're on" entails because college shows are *nothing* like doing stand-up at a club.

When you are booked at a college, there is no warm-up act. You, the first and only comic, go up to a stone-cold audience. And you must kill. No small chuckles or laughs. No do-overs.

You must slay, to both honor the craft and the people who selected you from NACA.

And how you do that night?

Just know that the success of your show will spread to other schools like wildfire.

Yes, all the schools talk to one another, like a fun tight family.

Anyway, congratulations! The show is over to wonderful reviews! Take a bow!

Now, don't forget to professionally celebrate with everyone at the venue.

Take lots of pictures with the students, and always thank them for an amazing time. Again, you were hand-selected to visit their campus, and they had plenty of other options to choose from.

But after a little schmoozing, the show is officially in the books. And I hate to be a buzzkill, but it's right back to the hotel.

Where, if you are smart, you will sleep as much as you can.

'Cause guess what? You have to do it all over again in the morning. Reverse that original ninety-minute drive back to that airport, return the car, take two more planes to the next city, get another rental car (man, Avis must really freakin' love us!), and find your next hotel.

With the same positive attitude.

And don't look now, but guess what? That entire summary of travel I just described—wait for it—was just for connecting the travel for two schools!

Yep. Just one twenty-four-hour cycle.

Fifty-one schools down. Sixty to go.

And that's how it was on my biggest tour to date—111 bookings.

I often wonder how my body and mind are still in one piece.

And the numbers get crazier.

But for the past twenty-five years—and I still can't believe it—I have averaged seventy schools per year since 1998.

That's right. Every year, without fail, seventy cities or more.

(And I'm still not used to comics around the country teasing me and calling me "the King of Colleges," especially since I still haven't seen any crown!)

But please know that there is zero arrogance here as I say this—because let me tell ya, as grateful as I am, I always remember two things: (1) God could take away this blessing from me at any time, and (2) after every tour, I know that I'm gonna need to feel born again, kinda like that scene with Tim Robbins in *Shawshank Redemption*. You know, the one when he crawls out of the old sewer pipe into the water, shedding his old, stinky clothes and raising his arms to the sky.

After a job well done, I need time to get my bearings again, catch my breath, and recharge with a short break.

But notice I said "short," because right around the corner, there is a new tour on the calendar, and

those dozens of airline tickets and car reservations won't just magically appear by themselves.

So even if you get your break, prepare to spend at least a few weeks plotting your next route, finding the best one-way tickets from city to city to city, and matching them up with car reservations when you land. (Oh, and try not to get charged a second day with a rental car by bypassing your flight time. It adds up, especially getting charged an extra seventy bucks a day when you miss the cutoff time by, get this, a slim ten minutes! Thanks, construction on the highway!)

Let's not forget about the mental preparation as well. Packing a bag for a month. Saying goodbye to everyone and everything that is normal to you. Managing your finances, your energy, and your sanity.

And oh yeah, there's the stress of coming up with new material.

(Now you know why us veteran comics sometimes roll our eyes at all the smiling, naive wise guys who ask, "So, are you doing any new stuff?")

Yeah, not this week . . .

Sometimes the mental prep is just about survival, and that absolutely includes preparing yourself for another mental aspect: isolation.

On the road, there's more than enough alone time.

Think about it. We don't get to travel with anyone as a comedian in this market. No fellow band members partying on tour buses. No companions or significant others to pass the time or bond with (that can get very expensive).

Now you know why I laugh at all the "business travelers" who complain about how their one flight this month got delayed twenty minutes and then post on social media, "Ahhhhhhhh! I can't stand airports!"

Or they complain about how the Marriott—you know, the fancy hotel with the marble floors and the grand piano that you can't touch—didn't have a spa, or how the filet mignon they ordered wasn't cooked properly, forcing them to "suck it up" by getting loaded up on booze with their office pals, which of course was charged to the company.

Life as a NACA comic isn't quite so glamorous. Often the only hotel in the small farm towns you visit is a lone Motel 6. Oh, and for dinner? Well, because the town is pretty much closed by the time you get out of the show at 9:00 p.m., it's also slim pickings. Try the twenty-four-hour truck stop an exit down the road for some rock-hard jerky and a dusty can of peas. You gotta stay healthy on the road after all.

And yes, yes, I hear the critics and doubters. "Enough of this negativity! It can't be like that every time!"

No, you're right. It's not. But when you do a large volume of schools in some harsh climates practically year round, what I just wrote is the rule rather than the exception.

"Oh, c'mon, Eric. Life can't be that bad on the road! What about mixing things up with some solo exploring? Geez, stop your whining, and get out there and make the most of these cities!"

Sigh. Don't you think I've thought of that? You see, my naive friend, there is literally no time for real sightseeing or going on a nature hike. Sometimes we are in a city for less than six hours—and that includes landing, showtime, and taking off again.

So, guess what the answer is when you excitedly ask, "Hey, did you get to climb the Arch in St. Louis, visit the zoo in San Diego, or catch that cool local band after the show?"

No, I didn't.

And for God's sake, the biggest I-wanna-rip-out-my-hair moment? (And I love to laugh and tease my friends about this!)

When I am doing my sixth city in a row and it's "just a thirty-five-minute drive" to your house for a quick dinner and hello. For the love of God, thank you, but I just can't—again. There is literally no time, and I value our friendship too much for you to invite a sleepwalking cesspool of "stinky poo" for dinner. I would've loved to see ya, but all jokes aside, us comics are hustling.

This career is so demanding, and as I like to put it, we are our own Swiss Army knives. We are our own writers, producers, directors, wardrobe people, promoters, travel agents, and social media updaters.

Never mind that I'm also a son, brother, uncle, and hopeful role model—all of which are even more important to me than anything else.

On the road, I'm doing the very best job I can for so many different people and in so many settings. And when it comes to comedy, unlike many other occupations, "You only get one shot," as the great philosopher Eminem once said. "Do not miss your chance to blow, 'cause opportunity comes once in a lifetime."

OK, young comics. I'm going to stop here, so listen to me.

Rejoice in all your bookings, and don't you dare lose sight of what you just accomplished at NACA!

But more so, get ready to build some of the most amazing relationships with some of the most wonderful advisers and students! I still cannot believe the wonderful people I get to call friends after twenty-five years, having actually had the pleasure of watching young freshmen grow up to have their own families and kids!

Yes, it's truly been such a blessed ride, and despite all the hard work and sacrifice involved, I wouldn't trade it for anything in the world. No way. And after all, isn't the success that comes from hard work what makes life so rewarding? I sure think so.

Oh! Wait, I almost forgot. One last thing. When you are out there on the road, of course I hope you stay safe and take care of yourself, but please use the travel time to process, reflect, recharge, and appreciate.

Appreciate how very special and unique this market is, and if you do the work and honor yourself along the way, it will leave you with some of the most remarkable memories and rewarding feelings that you could ever imagine.

Yes, ever!

And always know that if you ever need anything—because I have been there so many times over, in both the good times and the bad—I am always here for you. Got it?

Now then. Get outta here. Get out there. Enjoy, and trust yourself.

You've got this!

GOD DAMMIT, JUST DON'T SAY IT!

It takes a clean sixty minutes to do a great college comedy show, and it only takes ten seconds never to be asked back again." —Me

With over twenty-five years in the college comedy market, I've learned (the hard way) the importance of following that advice every time I hit the stage at a university.

The "hard way" came at an important NACA regional conference in the fall of 1999. I had just gotten a standing ovation and was just bursting with excitement at how well my showcase went.

"Yes! A standing ovation!" I said to my veteran agent and legend in this business, Mr. Joey Edmonds.

The very first thing he said back? "What. Were. You. Thinking?!"

"Wait, what?" I shot back, both a little confused and very confident—typical young, know-it-all comic.

"What was with all the 'goddamns'?"

Um, laughs and a standing ovation, I thought but was too respectful to say. But what the hell did he know anyway? He only had thirty years' worth of knowledge and experience in the market. And excuse me, friend, this is a new generation. My jokes and killer style won the day.

Turns out, I couldn't have been any more wrong. While saying I was being true to my—and I cringe at writing this—"artistic integrity," I was all about ego on that stage.

But my ego kept me from properly reading the crowd—in the Baptist South!

Yep, I was not only recklessly spewing blasphemy every fourth sentence, but also disrespecting my agency and all the other comics associated with the agency. Not a great way to do business.

Oh, and speaking of business, yeah, that suffered too. Although we did so-so with booking dates, we also left thirteen schools off the books, all because of the cocky and casual goddamns during my set.

At $2,500 a pop, I had just left $32,500 out there. That was $32,500 gone—in a mere fifteen-minute showcase—for doing it my way. (Sorry, Frank. Love the song, but it just doesn't work like that in this market.)

Now, before the comedy critics come charging with fire torches in hand, claiming that there is no right way to do comedy, that it isn't always about the money, or that so-called artistic integrity is way more important than sticking to a college show formula—let me say they are 100 percent, unequivocally right.

But I will say this too. In order to be successful in the college market, there are a few guidelines I follow—and note that I didn't say "rules," you frustrated, artistic skeptics out there.

I have merely compiled a "mental approach" over time and have made the personal choice to adhere to it as much as I can.

Now, why did I take this route, and why have I committed to it like I committed to my extra-small gold necklace in my model shoot and first headshot?

(And wait til' you see *that* headshot that screams the "Bad Boy of Figure Skating!")

Well, for that answer, you need to read on.

THE COLLEGE "CONTROVERSY"

In my first twenty years of playing colleges, other comics excitedly said "Wow, that sounds like fun! How can I get into that?"

But these last five years of performing at colleges? Most comics give me a sarcastic grimace, followed by a definitive "Oh, hell no!" or "Those students are way too hypersensitive and politically correct for me!"

Well, I have some opinions on this, and that's exactly what they are, just opinions.

I do not want to lump anyone in just one category, whether it be comics or universities, as every situation is different. But from my travels, I can definitely tell you that this "hot topic" is not just black and white. In fact, there is a lot of fascinating gray in the middle.

Let me break them down into some thematic categories for the purpose of this discussion.

Age

The first concept that I'd like you to consider is, very simply, the age factor. And by no means am I making a disparaging comment on the intellect of students. As a matter of fact, many of them are way above where I was at their age.

But the fact of the matter is, the students—your crowd—are only eighteen to twenty-one years old. They have comparably limited life experience, and experience is absolutely irreplaceable. There simply is no substitute for it.

Why?

Comedically speaking, many students at that age just don't have the personal reference points to fully appreciate certain jokes, sometimes even jokes and teasing that are boldly delivered with heavy doses of sarcasm.

But there's more to consider about this crowd.

Who is actually at your show? Well, certainly not the students out at the frat party getting crazy. No, you're crowd, for the university's clean Friday-night alternative to partying (using the words many advisers have chosen) often include the "shy" and "socially awkward."

Think about it.

A lot of them might have never had sex before!

Heck, they can't legally drink.

And think of all the other life experience they have not yet had either. They've never lived on their own. They've never paid for a stack of bills. They've not spent years working in an office.

So where does that leave your joke about punching out early, using your tax refund on a bottle of whiskey, and then hurrying home to hit up that hot girl on Tinder who you hope to bang from behind?

Exactly, it probably won't fly …

Again, let me be clear. I am not calling college students babies or naïve. They don't need to be coddled. But c'mon. Follow me on this.

It's like driving a car. After years of driving experience (there's that word again), we now speed, drive with one hand, and cut corners—sometimes literally. I know I do. But when you are first learning to drive, it's hands at ten and two, obeying the speed limit, and looking both ways at all times.

As the comic, *you're riding shotgun next to these "new drivers."* So to even insinuate doing anything differently, such as offering a racy joke or opinion that they are totally clueless about, will cause them to lock up and want to pull the car over . . . for the rest of your set.

And the result?

A terrible show and an awful review that again spreads like wildfire to other colleges.

OK, I'll take some questions. Yes, you.

"So, wait a minute, Eric. What the hell then am I supposed to talk about in my act at a college? And for an *hour*?"

Just do what you feel is appropriate. And as I always say, just do you.

But please know that when I say that, it is *not* an excuse to do shock humor or push buttons just for the sake of pushing buttons. It's also not an excuse to dive in to your hipster NYC or LA set because you are "honest" and "just speaking the truth."

Because to them, it is simply your truth and, again, one they can't fully process yet or, worse, might view as inappropriate and disastrously unfunny.

Thanks for the question. Yes, another question in the back?

"But isn't performing about being able to express yourself? Screw that, man! I'm going to be an artist who doesn't compromise my beliefs!"

OK, terrific. I'm genuinely happy for you. But please know this. Although the college stage is a wonderful place to creatively vent and "inform," that kind of act is simply not going to be fully received or even appreciated by students who are just out of high school. Again, most of them are eighteen years of old and usually from a rural farm town like North Platte, Nebraska! (Yes, after playing all fifty states a few times over, I can tell you that this is your audience. Other than the major cities and the coasts, most of America is made of small-town folks living rural lifestyles.)

And that brings me to my second point.

Fresh Out of High School

Remember senior year in high school? I actually don't want to. Remember how my first date was my senior prom? Sigh.

For you, though, senior year was probably a time of letting loose, celebrating, and being the self-appointed king or queen of the castle. Oh yeah, life operated on your terms. And in some ways, you were the coolest, most untouchable person on Earth.

Your rules, your way!

But having made August college orientations my specialty in the college market, I've seen plenty of too-cool-for-school students forced to shed those letter jackets and enter a whole new world back at the bottom of the totem pole.

The looks on their faces are absolutely priceless. They're all nervous, quiet, uncertain, and petrified—and in some cases, tears are naturally shed while saying goodbye to Mom and Dad.

Indeed, becoming a college freshman is a deer-in-the-headlights moment. Heck, I don't think I even slept at all my first night.

But here's where I'm making my point. Though the students may be nervous about the next four years, it's college that steps in to save the day! They open up their world, offering students confidence, new values, more maturity, and most of all, *accountability*.

From the get-go, colleges make it clear that it is time to grow the hell up. And as a student, you better bring it every day because although colleges want you to experience the greatest time of your life, they have no qualms with testing every ounce of your physical and emotional being.

That's right.

It's no longer your rules, your way.

It's university rules, university way.

This new reality forces students to rethink their world in an important, fundamental way. Suddenly you are forced to treat others with more respect, to see the world outside yourself, and to expand your mind to see and experience different cultures and lifestyles. College is a place with zero tolerance for immaturity and disrespect.

And here's where you come in as a comic. When you perform for this age group of eighteen- to twenty-one-year-olds who want to fit in and be seen in this new positive light, it is very easy then to have a joke or concept go against what the students and the university are trying to build together.

When you come to a campus—into that new world with all its rich traditions, sports teams, alumni, and an environment built around a rock-solid, uplifting way of thinking—and tell a *joke that runs counter to what everyone else is trying to achieve together,* even if you think the joke is incredible, it is you, the foolish comic, who stands alone.

So just please just be aware of that.

Digital Generation

There is another psychological element going on when I observe college campuses, especially now that I am playing for an entirely new generation of people younger than myself.

Yes, time is flyin' by and I'm getting old. (Oh, shut up.)

So allow me to offer an observation that several others have stated. Today, with our technology, gadgets, apps, Amazon, Grubhub, and FaceTime, we really don't even have to leave the house if we don't want to. This is the world that this young generation is growing up in, and many live without having to expend as much effort as those in older generations. Today, it's all about the luxuries: fancy bottled water over drinking out of the "dirty" faucet, smartphones over landlines, and tapping an iPad over rewinding a cassette tape with a pencil.

Not only are things "easier" for the youngsters now, but the variety of options before them is freakin' off the charts. For every one thing we were "forced" to play or live with, they have with forty-nine different options and—needless to say—much better options. So, on paper, you can see why so many people adopt the narrative that this younger generation has it so easy, are so "spoiled," and have no idea what it is like to really "struggle."

But here's my theory. Although that argument has merit, I will firmly go on record to say this outcome is *not* necessarily the kids' fault.

C'mon, let's be fair. People are constantly reproducing, and it is no child's fault that they were born in this particular era! I mean, I wouldn't want to be called soft for not having served in World War II! (But I have. Thanks, Gramps.)

Young people's response to this "soft" narrative is fascinating, too.

I have noticed on campuses that students are more than well aware of how their generation is viewed. Not only are many frustrated with this depiction of who they are, even more don't know what to do about it.

This brings me to my point.

In some ways, I think this new generation is on a search for an *identity*. Imagine being an eighteen-year-old or a twenty-one-year-old trying to fit in, figure out a career path, and keep up with school—all while trying to figure themselves out amid an endless sea of options and messages surrounding them at every turn. There's all the gadgets, all the dislikes, all the judgmental tweets, all the videos, all the input from us "older" folks. Self-doubt seems inevitable, especially without the experience to properly process everything.

So yeah, being young in today's world can lead to a very unclear existence at times. Again, I'm not trying to speak for all students, but it's incredible what some of them have said to me.

"Geez, man. I don't even know who I am sometimes."

"Sometimes I don't even feel like I *have* a direction."

"I can't even keep track of everything. I mean, sometimes I don't even know what to do with all of this information. It's definitely a lot of pressure to keep up with."

So hell, if you don't say it, I will! *I do not envy them.* At least my generation gets to experience this unheard-of amount of options with much more mature minds.

They don't have that luxury.

And again, I'm not making excuses for them. Those who know me know that I hate excuses.

But looking back on my life and who I was back then, I *know* I would not be able to handle this kind of world so easily! No way, not at all . . .

That eighteen-year-old-Eric? Please! He was too insecure, too shy, too introverted, and a major perfectionist. And trust me, that last one can be a serious problem with all the options there are to getting something "perfectly right."

To be blunt again, I think this generation feels the dual pressure of trying to figure themselves out (which is challenging for all of us) *while* trying to avoid all the unnecessary self-esteem–damaging hype and bullshit.

And there is a lot of it out there, people—a lot more than we had. Plus they are the generation that also now has to deal with climate change, astronomically high student loans, and tons of plastics destroying our oceans and wildlife, all cozily wrapped in a gazillion-dollar deficit.

Ah, yes, here come the critics. "Damn, Eric! This is just the type of attitude that has created this unappreciative, spoiled, entitled generation! We are babying them to death and creating a world full of pansies!"

No, we are not, and here's my main point.

Although there is a certain percentage of young college students who keep falling into the trap of immaturity, uncalled-for spoiled behavior, and weaker dispositions—which definitely is so freakin' annoying!—this is not true across the board.

Hell, even as I write this chapter, the entire country—led by a powerful, mature, inspired, and proactive youth—has united together to protest the sickening George Floyd murder! From major cities to the smallest of towns, I am so honored to watch this generation lead the charge to condemn racism and systematic oppression. This generation, like all the ones before it, is reaching toward a greater purpose. Incredible! I'm so proud and thankful!

And here's some more food for thought . . .

One of the more obvious reasons why our youth are sometimes seen as incredibly uptight—wait for it—is that they are trying to mimic the world *us adults have created!*

Look around. They are simply trying to fit in a world with these new politically correct "rules." And they see messages of these rules everywhere; on campus, on TV, on the streets, and all over social media. And who put them there? Us! The adults! The ones who are supposed to be setting an example about how to have even just a little bit of a sense of humor and lighten the heck up!

So we can't blame the students entirely.

Here's a lovely example of that.

I remember doing a sold-out club on a Friday night—so no, not a college crowd. I was telling a nice story about how I gave a college sweatshirt from my thank-you gift bag to the housekeeper at my hotel. After performing at hundreds of colleges, I didn't necessarily need it, and it might be something nice for the housekeeper to wear themselves.

For this bit, I did both my voice and the housekeeper's voice. The crowd awed at the gesture and then totally laughed at our interaction, amazing chemistry, and the punch line. The bit went so well and had nothing but good intentions.

Hooray, right?

Well, after the show, a woman came up to me very pissed off and said, "Hey, Eric. Great show, but um … can I ask you something?

I said sure.

"So why did the housekeeper have to have a *Spanish* accent? That's stereotyping!"

Even now, it makes me crazy to even just think about this.

After pausing for a good five seconds, using a smile to stifle my frustration, I said as nicely as I could, but definitely raising my voice, "Why did I use a Spanish voice, you ask, ma'am? BECAUSE SHE *WAS* SPANISH! THAT'S WHO SHE WAS!"

She stared on, horrified.

"Oh my God! It wasn't a *Russian* housekeeper!" Then, doing my best Russian accent, I really leaned in to the sarcasm. "D'you need *frish* towwwwel? Son of a b., she was Spanish, dammit. SPANISH!"

Don't worry. I softened the blow with a giggle.

The woman just nervously smiled, realizing that she just made a complete fool of herself for being overly analytical and overly sensitive. And there we were at the back bar and in front of half the crowd cheering me on.

So, it is not just the college students.

And although everyone is their own individual, I really do think that, in some ways, the students see what the world has become and are merely trying to do their best to mimic.

And look, concerning the poor lady at the club. Don't get me wrong. I think it's wonderful how so many great causes are happening in the world about respecting human rights. We have come one hell of a long way as a society! Everyone deserves to be happy, love who they want, and be treated equally.

But as with anything, too much sensitivity can be overkill, and we can lose the very essence that keeps us all thriving and growing—namely, things like patience, tolerance of different opinions, and most of all, listening to each other.

That's right. We don't *listen* anymore. We have become a society that just wants to be right, so we point fingers and divide each other up into more subsets than this world needs. Look, we don't always have to agree with each other, but that doesn't necessarily mean that the sky is falling.

And it especially doesn't mean that disagreeing with someone means that you hate them!

We really have to calm down a little bit and simply take the most logical and healthy approach: to strike a chord of respect, common sense, decency, and balance; to converse, learn, disagree, agree, and find a way to bend but not break; and to stay true to who you are while inspiring rather than criticizing.

Look, I know this chapter won't necessarily change the world or bring peace to foreign countries. (And It wasn't supposed to.)

But I really hope it touches at least one person, helping them stay true to themselves while finding one, just one, commonality with someone different than themselves, spreading the love and tolerance that this world desperately needs.

Just as important, *learning how to laugh at yourself and lighten the hell up!*

Just a bit. (*Wink.*)

OK, I'm off my tiny soapbox.

Let's now get back to your career and address the important question here: Should you play the college market? Do you even want to?

Well, only you can answer that.

But I sincerely hope that I have brought some clarity by sharing my experience here.

And in the meantime, always remember.

Attitude is so powerful.

Life is so short.

Tread lightly, everyone.

SPEAK NOW OR FOREVER HOLD YOUR PEACE

I have said a lot so far, especially about the college market. Now I want to devote a separate chapter to explaining just a little more about why I work this amazing platform, what I get from it, and where I see it going.

And I'll be blunt here because I care so much about not only what I do, but the craft of comedy as a whole.

So, first of all, I didn't choose the college market. It chose me. After some referrals by some wonderful comics that I looked up to, working with colleges, thankfully, fell right into my lap.

One night, I simply got asked to play my very first university, and as with any promising new relationship, the chemistry was undeniable.

Sticking with the metaphor, I fell in love, and we will be celebrating our twenty-seventh anniversary in 2020. (I love you, sweets!)

When I say there was an undeniable chemistry, I am talking about an effortless back and forth where the audience and I just naturally clicked. (So, in other words, I never *purposely* wrote stand-up for a college audience.)

Why?

Because my material already seemed to connect with that audience. I've never had to dramatically alter my hour-long show so that I would be accepted and applauded by college students and their advisers.

And to be blunt, I never ever think I "sold out"—to conform, obey, or kiss butt—for *anybody*. That is not who I am. Growing up, I learned very quickly that you must rely on yourself and be proud of who you are.

There is zero time for doing something halfway.

What you see me do on and off the stage is 100 percent me, and that is being silly, observational, and frustratedly unfortunate. There are also healthy doses of mimicking, acting out human behaviors, singing, and venting—and yes, completely randomly.

And the really cool part?

I actually have seen the growth in my comedic voice subtly change along my journey. I went from being the cool, young guy who is merely silly with the students to a more mature, honest, big-brother figure who takes pride in sprinkling words of wisdom and lessons on accountability—all wrapped up in a high energy routine where I am the one to laugh at and laugh with.

If that is not being authentic on stage, I don't know what is.

Now, are there more cutting-edge comics? Of course. Comics who embrace being more gruffly opinionated? Without a doubt. But again, I never and—will never—view myself as doing a lighter style of comedy that cautiously peddles fluff and commentary on "safe" topics. Neither of those truly exist.

Comedy is comedy, and even if it "feels safe," no sooner will you find out that it's not.

Those who follow me on social media (or read the last chapter) know I have many opinions on big topics such as faith, race, economics, and lifestyle.

But for some reason (and this is important) when I am doing a college gig, I have too much fun embracing a comedic style that builds during the show to challenge the students, make them think, and teach them to laugh at themselves.

By the end, they don't even realize that, while they were laughing, they learned some very important and timeless life lessons—the ones that made my experience in college oh-so fulfilling.

I revel in the fact that, in one night of performing, I just had the honor of changing people's lives for the better, even if just a little bit.

And although the standing ovations and amazing reviews mean a job well done, I simply cannot explain how more rewarding those things feel when you know that you positively touched someone's life.

When you really think about it, that is all anyone could ever ask for as a performer—never mind as a human being.

THERE'S NO PLACE LIKE HOME

It's no secret that people enter comedy for that raw love of the stage, the crowd, and the jokes. But then reality sets in, and you realize it doesn't pay very well, if at all.

So on every drive home to my cockroach studio apartment in Milwaukee, eager for my gourmet ketchup sandwich (and again, it is actually quite good if you get the right bread), I'd be lying if I said I never thought about when I might get my big break.

Today, twenty-four years later, I'm still pinching myself that it happened, and I am so, so thankful to God for it.

The story goes something like this.

On August 9, 1996, I found myself at home in New Haven, Connecticut, helping clear out some boxes for my mom who was ready to sell the family home and start a journey out west. Don't ask me why, don't ask me when, but the good Lord gave me two things that day: confidence and boredom.

As I took a break moving old clothes and furniture, I remember being so excited about a few new bits and the solid twenty minutes I had to my name (not that either could buy me a cup of coffee). While sitting in the director's chair in the kitchen (maybe the chair was an omen?), I decided to call my good friend Eddie in New York City. I had just emceed for Eddie a few weeks before, and I knew he ran a new-talent night at Caroline's on Broadway in Midtown.

With my new material, I was ready! Well, not really.

THE RICHEST COMEDIAN YOU'VE NEVER HEARD OF

I nervously asked over the phone, "Hey, Eddie. It's Eric O'Shea. Is there any way to be a part of the Monday new-talent show sometime?"

Being a legend in NYC and a great soul, he said, "Sure, pal, but you have to bring about ten people. The club won't allow just anyone to go up. You have to support the club with the usual ticket money and by buying drinks and all that. But there is a spot open next Monday."

Fast-forward to August 19, 1996.

So with nothing to lose—and to be honest, not realizing how monumental this opportunity was—I rallied seven family members, two friends, and my girlfriend, Kristen, who took a bus all the way from Philadelphia just to support me.

I remember walking inside this Mecca of comedy in awe at all the pictures on the wall, all the people who had graced the stage, and (*gulp*) the three hundred people in the audience excitedly supporting the other raw new talent that could be the next big thing.

Was I nervous? A little. But for some reason, I had a perfect combination of excited anxiety and eagerness. Like many young comics with a false sense of security, I thought my twenty minutes of material was ready for television. If *you* believe it, that's all that matters, right?

So while the other fourteen comics did some great NYC bits about subways, traffic, relationships, and "spicy" opinions, I found myself doing my best ten minutes on my strict mom and her wooden spoon, being a little kid pouting, some self-deprecating observations, Hermie the Elf from *Rudolph the Red-Nosed Reindeer*, and my closer—the cast of *Seinfeld* as if they were all in kindergarten.

Now keep in mind, what is amazing about this closer is not so much me imitating all four voices in a tiny classroom, but the fact that the bit itself came about during one of the worst shows I have ever done in my life. I was eating it on stage like I'd never eaten it before! You see, a month prior I was opening up for my friend Fred while on a Midwest hell tour of bars and restaurants, and in good ol' North Platte, Nebraska, I was at some "club bar" just *dying* on stage and more than ready to bail.

But just before I did, I asked Fred, who was in the back of the room, "Hey, should I do the *Seinfeld* voices I did in the car on the way here?"

He did his trademark mellow smirk and grunted, "Yeah!"

So with nothing to lose, I imitated the cast of *Seinfeld* as if they were in kindergarten: Jerry excited, George upset he didn't get a pumpkin sticker, Elaine shocked by poor George, and Kramer, of course, eating the glue.

It was a hit.

The place went wild, and I salvaged any last piece of dignity I had in order to sleep well in the forty-dollar motel—with HBO and color TV, as the sign said. (Trust me, this was an upgrade from sleeping on a rest area bench for six hours. True story.)

Anyway, back to Caroline's.

So there I was, in a packed club in New York City having just finished my set.

It was the best damn show I'd ever had.

It was one of those shows where everything you said, did, and *breathed* just oozed laughs, applause, and success.

Dammit, if we only had it on tape!

Oh, we did.

Unbeknownst to me, Eddie and company didn't want to tell me about the giant camera in the back taping all the comics—he "didn't wanna make me any more nervous."

So after saying good night in the mic, taking in all the applause, excitedly waving at my table of supporters in the front row, and chuckling at Eddie's sarcastic whisper in my ear, "Don't worry, Eric, you'll get 'em next time," I exited stage left.

There, smiling in front of me, were two very important people named Barry and Maureen, who would one day be my managers. I had zero idea how powerful they were. Hell, I wasn't experienced enough to know. So I simply shook their hands and exchanged contact info as if I was talking to a regular audience member just saying, "Nice job." I was far more excited to celebrate with my family and friends and toast the night at Odeon.

Little did I know that this brief encounter would change everything.

Fast-forward to August 26, 1996, in Akron, Ohio.

Now, as with most things in this business, a wonderful, amazing night on stage is just that—one night. That applause you hear just means it's time to hit the road and prove your worth again.

For this week, my girlfriend, Kristen, was tagging along, riding the high from Caroline's with me and joining me for another adventure. This time, though, I found myself middling at a club where the owner didn't have a hotel for me (again), so there we were all weekend, *in the storage room of the club*, on a mattress next to a big box of Solo cups and beer kegs.

Every so often, staff would open the door to get stuff as Kristen and I made out and tried to plan our next move together. Really fun. (At least we didn't have to go far to get to the club for the show.)

And then it happened—the moment that would change my career, my life, my outlook, and my destiny.

Someone opened the door to the storage room, a.k.a. my penthouse suite, and said, "Eric, you have a phone call at the pay phone in the lobby."

Seeing the receiver dangling upside down, I picked it up and asked, "Hello?"

It was then that I heard a monologue that I'll never forget.

"Hello, Eric? It's Maureen, the one you met coming off stage at Caroline's last week. Are you sitting down?"

"Uh, yes?" I wasn't.

"I just sent the tape of your amazing set at Caroline's to ABC-Disney, who wants to give you a holding deal for $125,000. You don't even have to audition again, as only you and Joe Rogan have ever been offered a deal like that from a ten-minute videotape. Can you be in NYC next week to meet? Barry and I would love to sign you, get things going, and be your managers."

I couldn't believe what I was hearing. My life *literally* changed, as they say, overnight—in the lobby of a comedy club where I slept in the storage room.

Now, I won't bore you with the details of all the phone calls and happy tears, or all the amazing comics who told audiences about what had just happened (I will forever be grateful for that).

And I won't bore you with how I was still so "disciplined" and "focused" that I didn't even know how to celebrate that weekend. (After all, I was on a budget.)

But I will tell you that, in the blink of an eye, when the chips are down, all it takes is some reflection, confidence, twenty minutes of material, and some luck to have your comedy journey change forever.

But if I'm being completely honest? Hell, I still can't explain it.

That on one magical night, in front of my most precious loved ones, in front of three hundred strangers, and with a gigantic camera rolling, everything just fell into place—the way that it was supposed to, I guess.

August 19, 1996, a day that will forever live in my heart, and one that I thank God for *every damn day.*

Oh, and if anyone needs any help moving boxes out of their home . . .

You know who to call.

WHAM BAM, THANK YOU, SPAM

We've all gotten that inbox reminder after signing up for something online. "If you do not see our email, please check your spam folder."

But what about if you are not even expecting an email?

Be honest. How often do you actually check your spam folder? Once a week? Twice a week? Only when you are wanting to delete the dozens of annoying product offers, financial scams, and porn sites that somehow found your Gmail account?

Well, on this particular afternoon, I've come out of the swimming pool, am back in the house with my nephew hanging on my leg, and am dying to go back to the pool. I check my email and then—don't ask me what prompted me to do it—decide to open that all-important spam folder.

And every day I thank the good Lord that I did (and without automatically clicking Delete All in one fell swoop).

That's right. In between the two spam emails with the headlines "The Best Pet Stain Carpet Cleaner" and "Need a Bigger Penis?" was an invitation to not only attend but also *perform* at the Creative Arts Emmy Awards in Hollywood, California.

Wait, what?

This has to be a scam or a joke, I thought. Maybe they just want a donation?

So, taking my finger off the Delete All button, I nearly exploded with manic delirium.

It was true. This was real.

On September 9, 2009, the producer of the Creative Arts Emmy Awards wanted me to join the stars and legends of television to perform a clean, abbreviated version of my closing bit "Songs for Commercials."

Now I won't bore you with how I spent the next month giddy every day leading up to the event, bought my black Calvin Klein tuxedo, or managed to squeeze my cheeks back together after smiling all the time.

But I was ready. I had been *dying* to do something like this. And to do it on the biggest stage with the legends I grew up watching was even more happy-tear inducing than I could have ever imagined.

After flying out for my rehearsal and practicing my seven clean songs for a Hollywood crowd, I couldn't wait to do it again, only for real this time.

And I had no idea how incredible it would be.

Oh, it was the whole nine yards. Maybe even ten.

The red-carpet entrance, the photographers, the flash bulbs popping, and even my very own handler whose job it was, according to her, to "follow you around, at all times, like a shadow, making sure you always have everything you need. Water, tissue, pecans …"

(Pecans? Um, OK. Not sure where that came from, but I love pecans!)

So there I was in the green room, all dressed up and ready to go, hair and makeup done, with my mom as my date to thank her for all her support growing up and being my biggest fan.

Now what? Preshow pictures? Sure, I'd love that!

Wowza! I found myself taking pics with stars like Ryan O'Neal, Katey Segal, and one of my favorites, the legendary Carol Burnett. She was so kind, so respectful and treated me like we were old friends. And I simply just *had* to tell her, "Forget *SNL*, forget *Mad TV*. I'm sure you know this, Mrs. Burnett, but what you did—every week—with Bob Mackie's costumes and Broadway-play-quality sketches was, without a doubt, the absolute real deal. No one—no one—will come close to doing what you all did. And now, before I say thank you, um, could ya ..."

She smiled, anticipating the request she'd heard thousands of times before.

"Could you just tug on your ear for me?"

She let out a huge laugh, and she did. And just like that, I got goosebumps. I was seven years old again, watching her on CBS in my living room.

How could you top that, right?

Well, it kinda happened ...

As I was taking my seat in the front row, where they sat some of the people who would be called up to perform, there she was.

Wait, it couldn't be ... seated just a few seats away—from me?

I couldn't move. My hands are even shaking as I type this.

Who was it?

Only one of the greatest TV actresses that ever lived—a legend with decades of success that have won her admiration, love, and pure awe. She's known for more roles, more game-show appearances, and more iconic characters that will live in infamy than any other comedian.

We *all* know her.

My Golden Girl, the great, the timeless, the unmatched—Betty White!

I don't remember much about what I said. I was too nervous, with actual tears in my eyes from excitement. (Yes, it's a real thing!) At best, it was some combination of fumbling words that sounded like "Excuse me, Mrs. White. May I please take just one picture with you before we start? Oh, and do you remember the episode where you all went bowling, and you wanted to win the trophy so badly?"

Smooth, Eric. Smooth. I'm sure she's *never* been asked *that* before.

But she replied in her sweet, perky tone, "Well, of *course* I do, sweetheart!"

I put my arm around her—her shoulder just as solid as anything and everything she's ever done—and the moment was captured on film, in my mind, and in my heart. Forever.

The lights dimmed.

Snap out of it, Eric! It's showtime! You've got a job to do!

After taking my seat—again, in the front!—my handler said, "I am going to sneak down and get you fifteen minutes prior to you going on stage."

I was ready.

In fact, I wasn't nervous at all. I should have been, though, right? Why wasn't I? Sigh. Maybe it was the good luck from rubbing elbows with the *real* stars who would be on stage?

It didn't matter. Just as I was laughing at Seth MacFarlane and Tina Fey matching wits, I got a tap on the shoulder.

"Eric, it's time."

So with a deep breath, a smile, and a whisper to my mom—"Start the car, we may have to get out of here in a hurry"—I followed my handler backstage.

And man, did I learn in a hurry that damn does the show move fast! Amid all the staff, directors, producers, and writers were wires, cameras, cables, cues, and chaos. Each performer shared the same mic and traded it off like a freakin' baton. And at no time was there an empty stage. As one performer or beautiful person exited, another entered.

And then it was my turn.

THE RICHEST COMEDIAN YOU'VE NEVER HEARD OF

Fred Armisen handed me the mic and frustratedly said, "Wow, good luck. They are stiff."

Then, my cue: "And now, please welcome … Eric O'Shea!"

Well, the comedy gods were with me that night. I humbly strutted out, trying so hard to appear likeable and friendly. I was so honored, calm, and content. And to be honest, I never felt that I belonged on a stage with celebrities as much as I did that night.

I read my copy flawlessly, the music started, and I did my seven songs.

The crowd—again, an old Hollywood crowd probably asking, "Who in the hell is *this* guy?"—laughed, applauded, and made me feel like someone special.

After my songs, I read the nominees for Best Commercial, hence why they flew me out to do my commercial bit.

Then the lights went black, and the big screen popped up. And as I walked my way off stage feeling for the curtain, there was Kathy Griffin getting prepped for her turn.

"Very funny! Very funny, Mr. O'Shea!"

And just like that, it was over. Done. *Finito*. Mission accomplished. It was like getting off a roller coaster ride and wanting to do it again.

But that would have to wait for another day. At that point, I was on cloud nine and then suddenly rushed downstairs "to press." Now *completely* confused, I ask myself, "Wait, what am I pressing?"

I was told to stand on another red carpet and smile for dozens of photographers and flash bulbs popping. Like me at my senior *college* prom, it was so obvious that this was my "first time."

As I stood there giving them my best eighth-grade-school-picture smile (but thank God without my head resting on a closed fist), I was yelled at with enthusiasm to "mix it up" and "have some fun." After a few deep breaths, I let loose, spreading my arms out, making funny expressions, and of course, some sexy ones as if it was my own personal *People* magazine cover shoot.

We got a few good ones.

OK, *now* I was officially all done.

As Mom and I walked over to the Governor's Ball, chatting and walking the whole way with Louis C. K., we were so ready for an evening of food, fun, high fives, and reflection.

"Wow, did this just really happen? I mean, I think it did," my mind kept asking.

"Shhh … Just enjoy it, Eric. Don't ask any more questions."

That wiser voice inside me was content with just knowing that this was one of the most amazing nights of performing, camaraderie, high stakes, and personal achievements I have ever experienced.

As a gift, my mom gave me a giant picture of me in my tux as I was getting introduced and walked out on stage. It still hangs in my living room as a reminder of how amazing God is and how, for some reason, the stars aligned for one perfect night, allowing me to add a little of my own creativity to a show that needs no introduction.

And again, how it all came to pass? I still can't explain it.

All I know is that I am forever grateful for this experience that will stay with me forever and, needless to say, for the reminder that I should check my spam box a hell of a lot more often.

A DOSE OF REALITY . . . TV

So, I'm sitting in Austin, Texas, at one of my properties, and once again I've decided to check in with my main source for hot leads, a.k.a. my spam box.

This time, though, I decided to clean out my www.ericoshea.com website spam box, not from my AOL account. (Yes, I'm one of the last people who still has AOL. Dial-up is getting so annoying. *Screeeech, screeeech, bonga bonggggg!*)

And wouldn't ya know it? There it was a lone email sitting in the middle of more porn sites and bogus refinance plans.

A short note—from some scout who worked for *America's Got Talent*.

"I think you'd make a very good Texas comedian," he stated simply.

Again—wait, what?

What does that even *mean*? Texas comedian? OK, fine. I'm intrigued.

I write back, and he writes back, excitedly stating, "I watched a few clips of yours and want you to be on the show!"

Oh, c'mon. Another career moment surrounded by some incredible odds and a *spam box*?

Yep, I couldn't believe it either.

That on one boring afternoon, while sitting in my Austin condo, wondering whether I should do ten sit-ups or ten seconds of planks (neither of which I did), I got invited to fly out to Los Angeles, skip the audition process, and perform in front of the judges on *America's Got Talent*.

I was so excited.

And looking back, I was so unaware that this experience would be, by far, the most challenging thing I had ever tried to do.

Before I sum up my experience, I have to say that I hope this story translates well in the written word here, because as I type this you can't see my smiling or hear my chuckling, silly sarcasm, or moments of genuine sincerity.

And I kinda want you to.

This was one of my greatest accomplishments, and I am so proud of myself for following through and experiencing it. I learned so much on this adventure, including how to endure the unknown, how to write quickly, how to stand in the storm, and how to charge through every obstacle thrown my way.

This was an experience, as many of my friends told me, where my talent would be one of the *least* important factors in the advancement process.

The main variable that determined whether or not you moved on in the competition?

"Eric, along with your two-minute act, of course, you need *a fascinating storyline.*" I was told.

What does that even mean? I wondered. My bio? Where I was from? My favorite condiment? (BBQ sauce, for those playing at home)

Nope.

What the talent coordinator fervently told me was that I would need a story that would grab the audience and make them fall in love with me. That kind of story, fabricated or not, would get killer ratings and keep the audience at home rooting for me.

Acknowledging their advice, I created a narrative that highlighted what I valued most about myself. For TV, I'd be the likable guy who loved to mentor young comics and be the son that looked after his family.

And *why not* go with that, I thought? It's so easy to root for a guy like that. It also would allow people to see the sensitive side underneath the comic exterior.

Perfect! Now I just have to win them over with my material.

I was then told to create *four* different two-minute sets, and the producers and I would collaborate to decide on which set I'd do for the judges. Tricky, but doable.

I put together the best flow of what I thought was great stuff to choose from, and the producers loved all four options.

But I went for broke, campaigning for and finally winning out on showcasing my "hardest-hitting" stuff—my Hermie the Elf bit where I rapidly move my mouth like the cute, blonde Claymation character from *Rudolph the Red-Nosed Reindeer*, and my five funniest songs from my closer, "Songs for Commercials."

Great! With the set chosen, let's light this candle!

Well, not so fast.

And I really mean "not so fast."

Remember all the insane hurdles I mentioned earlier?

Well, here they come.

First of all, one hundred and twenty seconds is not much time to be funny, especially compared to acts with an immediate wow factor, like singing, magic, or acrobatics. You gotta hook 'em fast. And in the first minute of my two-minute set, the producers had chopped up my Hermie bit to basically zippo.

Adding to that, the song that I always end the Hermie bit with—Frank Sinatra's "My Way"—hadn't cleared copyright use.

Great. Well, at least the other sixty seconds of the audition—my high-energy, rapid-fire "Songs for Commercials" could still carry the act.

Woohoo!

Well ...

"Eric, we have a problem," the producer said. "We cannot use four of the five songs you selected. Absolutely not. As before, we cannot clear them for copyright purposes."

I was crushed. "But those are the best ones of my closer. Those are the sure-fire home-run hitters."

"Sorry, we just absolutely can't," she firmly stated again.

So, I was left with five of my "less-funny" song bits merely designed to be cutesy and used early on to show the audience how the bit worked, setting them up for the closers.

Well, I wasn't thrilled, but that's what I was left with—exactly two less-funny minutes for my audition.

For a month, I drove around town night after night, asking clubs to let me barge in on their weekend shows to rehearse the flow of my new, watered-down audition.

Then, yet again, I got another phone call.

"Eric, we have another issue."

Oh no. What?

"Well, we now cannot use the *actual artists* for the five songs you want to use"—wait for it—"so you will have to use cover band versions of the songs."

I wanted to die.

"But half of the humor comes from that *instant* recognition of the artist's actual voice, notes, beat, and oomph factor!" I argued.

"I'm sorry, Eric, but we simply cannot use the original artists for copyright clearance reasons," she said again without skipping a beat.

So, after listening to some of the worst covers of songs from the *already watered-down* version of what I originally wanted to do on stage, I had a decision to make.

Do I really want to move forward with this? Do I really want to show the judges, the crowd, and the nation something that isn't me, not to mention something that I am not very excited about?

Before I had made a decision, I got *another* phone call.

"Eric, the last song we chose? We now have to fully replace it, as it is not in our library of cover bands."

So there I was, all dressed up on a Friday night, in my car, literally driving to a club that took *forever* to book, all to rehearse an audition with a now-unusable song that was already burned onto a CD.

I'll admit it. I just pulled over on the side of the road, put my head on the steering wheel, and felt absolutely defeated. Why even go to the club and rehearse this set if I can't even use the song at the end—a.k.a. the main punchline and the closer to my closer?

I turned around and just drove back home.

And this went on for *four more weeks*, call after call, night after night.

All in all, I tried eleven songs for Viagra, and all eleven got rejected by the show—again, some on the way to the club, some even a day after getting tons of laughs.

Frustrating?

Yes, and I was at my wits end. But I still wasn't willing to give up.

Then came the day to fly out and do what they wanted me to do. I hopped on a flight, armed with a very odd rendition of what I considered not really me.

But my gut feeling and healthy pride wouldn't let me walk away from this, not now. Not after two months of constant editing, re-editing, clashing opinions, and frustrating setbacks.

So screw it. Let's do this.

I arrive at check-in and sign all the waivers, including one that asked, "If you have a medical emergency and collapse unconscious, do we still have the right to film you?"

Sure, why not.

I then got ushered to my holding room—that famous holding room—where all of the acts hang out.

With a just bagel and a carton of juice, I would then spend—wait for it—the next ten and a half hours waiting to go up.

Yep, *ten and a half hours of waiting*, with cameras constantly rolling to collect footage of all the nervous, sweaty, young hopefuls rehearsing.

It was the funniest collection of people you could ever see, by the way. People with pets, foreign acrobatic troupes, Hollywood mom's putting even more makeup on their minor daughter's already triple-coated face. It was a riot. People-watching at its finest!

There were dogs barking, people flipping, singers crooning, and I swear, I think I saw some guy shitting crayons in the corner. Now that's talent!

And remember how I mentioned earlier about how having a story was just as important as what you actually did on stage? Well, I forgot to mention that if they didn't like yours, or if it was too bland, they would just give you a "better" one!

That's right. So after they ditched my original, I no longer was just Eric O'Shea, nice-guy mentor. My new "persona" would be—brace yourself—a forty-something-year-old mama's boy comic who couldn't find love!

(Actually, not too far from the truth, but I digress. Please stop smiling!)

So for the next eight hours, the director had me wander about that tiny holding room to grab footage of me eyeing up women, aggressively flirting, and primping in the mirror with those Hollywood dressing-room lightbulbs. After all, my one goal was to find love, and all of this was totally normal behavior for finding a bride.

So I play along. Why not? I did my best cocky yet always-striking-out character. After a while, though, the whole phony charade just started to feel shallow and silly.

THE RICHEST COMEDIAN YOU'VE NEVER HEARD OF

And then it was 10:00 p.m. I realize how tired—actually, exhausted—I am and start wondering what the heck was going on.

Ah, but that's when I remembered the warnings from friends who had done the show before.

They want you to sweat it out.

With the cameras rolling, they can get anything and everything to make you look "uncomfortable." After all, it makes great television, right?

Sitting there at my wits end, wondering whether I will make my flight home the next day, all of a sudden an assistant producer squats down by my side, lights and cameras rolling to get my reaction.

She meekly smiles and says, "Oh, Eric. We may not have time to get you up tonight. The judges are getting tired, and we may strike the set. Is there *any* way you can come back tomorrow?"

Are you seriously kidding me?

With my best smile, and trying not to show any frustration (my very best acting job to date), I firmly looked at her and the cameras and let out a polite but obvious, "Noooo."

Well, something must have clicked in her head that I was really losing interest because about ten minutes later, I got "the call."

They wanted me on the set, ready to go on!

So with the cameras still rolling and following me from behind, I was led upstairs to the side of the stage, where someone was already performing in front of one of the biggest crowds and in one of the most beautiful theaters I have ever seen. Down in front, Simon Cowell, Howie Mandel, Heidi Klum, and Mel B sized up the guy, who was doing very well.

Then I heard the *X* buzzer.

BZZZZZ!!!

Now, I've heard loud things before: jackhammers, jet planes, that club owner and his gal on New Year's.

But this was by far one of the loudest sounds—and symbols of rejection—that I had ever heard in my life! It was almost as if they did it just to show me that I had entered the arena.

But it didn't faze me. Honestly, not at all, especially not after everything I'd gone through to get to this point.

Like a cocky cow being led to slaughter, I just smiled at the guy in front of me waiting to go on.

And confident I was. I've always wondered why. Was it my veteran experience, knowing that most of the acts were so new and younger than me? Or was I just so damn numb from waiting over ten hours and reworking my act dozens of times? I don't know.

But I was *so* confident that a producer saw me and asked, "Hey, can we get some footage of you preparing to go on?"

"Of course!" I whispered back.

With my best Rocky imitation, I winked at the cameras and shadow-boxed with a few uppercuts as I waited for my shot at becoming the proverbial champ.

"Cut," the producer whispered. "Wait. Eric, can you act more *nervous*? Like, can you wring your hands together like you are sweating?"

"But I'm not nervous," I calmly said with a smirk.

"OK, let's forget that, Eric. How about you sit next to him," she said, pointing to the other performer about to go on. "Then recite the line"—wait for it—"'Hey, are you nervous too? I hear that Simon is *really* in a bad mood.'"

(I'm chuckling again, but you're used to it by now)

So I did it. Without making a fuss, I did exactly what they told me to do. (*Cue the eye rolls.*)

After the act in front of me did his thing—I think it was the guy who quickly yanked a tablecloth off his naked body while lying down and without cracking a dish)—it was my turn!

I found myself standing next to Tyra Banks, and just trying to be polite, I said that it was nice to meet her.

The security didn't like that apparently, and he sternly told me, "Do not look or talk to her, please!"

No problem, I thought. (*Second eye roll.*)

So there I was, stage left, just waiting to be cued to walk out on stage.

This was it!

I could not believe all that had led up to this point. After finding a funny spam email in my Austin condo and then spending hours on the phone with producers, it was finally showtime!

A loud voice yelled at the crowd, "Quiet on the set!" and the judges returned from their water break and had makeup reapplied.

"Three, two, one … and go!" the stage manager said to me, escorting me by the arm.

I took my mark on the *X* at center stage—that *X* I'd seen so many times on television.

"I'm actually here," my mind said.

Heidi then brought me out of my head. "Well hello there. Tell us your name and what you are going to do for us today."

I did so … and then just continued to talk, offering up a completely random, unprepared comment.

"First of all, I just want to thank the judges for having me, as well as all these wonderful people out in the audience," I said, gesturing my hands out to the packed crowd and balcony above.

I will never forget Simon's face in that moment. He was simply enamored. I really can't describe it, but there was a look in his eye, an expression he gave me, that silently said, "I have no idea who this guy is, but what a classy thing to say, and I love him already."

It was the same type of look a proud father gives his son. I suddenly felt not only confident but appreciated as well.

And so I jumped into my two minutes, the culmination of weeks of frustration, hard work, excitement, and now joy to be there.

And I had them from the get-go with Hermie. Howie even turned to his left to smile and laugh with the other three judges. Then came "My Way," which finally got cleared because I was the one singing it. No, wait. I *belted* it out—as you get only one shot to do this—while frantically moving my mouth and smiling.

The crowd went nuts. They even stopped me from continuing with one of the most gratifying applause breaks I have ever received in all my years . . .

I beamed. Was this really happening?

OK, one bit down, one to go. And I couldn't wait.

It was time to do the songs.

I do the intro, and the music starts. I act out my songs for commercials, and on the final one, with the music still blasting, the crowd went wild. I flicked my hand skyward for a final ta-da, and then it happened.

I'd be lying if I said I wasn't hoping for it—something that I see on TV all the time and use to measure the success of each show.

I got a standing ovation!

This one was so different from the one's I'd received before. I had never experienced it before in this type of venue or when the stakes were so high—nothing at this level.

The crowd thunderously jumped to their feet—from the front, to the middle, to the back, to the balcony.

I couldn't believe what I was seeing. They were all going insane—and I made them that way!

It was one of the most gratifying moments I've ever had on a stage. And hey, not one buzzer either! (Although, Mel B didn't look super thrilled, but the producers told me she wasn't too popular with the staff and couldn't stand *anyone*.)

Coming off the stage, I was absolutely beaming. Everyone congratulated me: the staff, the producers, the point people, my go-to person. It was like hitting a walk-off home run.

"Eric! You nailed it!" one top producer said. "Do you know how hard it is to get a *standing O* here? As a comic? In two minutes? With this picky crowd and judges?"

I just smiled, so humbled.

At home, I was still elated about the audition and fell to my knees, thanking God for the incredible experience!

And I then got asked by the producers to send my *next* two minutes of material to show the judges. I was on top of the world. One producer even sent me a text telling me that they were all cracking up at those next two minutes and couldn't wait to see it live!

I walked around Scottsdale on cloud nine.

But hours passed into days—into a week to be exact.

I hadn't heard any update about my date to perform.

Then I get the email, and this is it verbatim:

Eric ... I have some bad news ... although you were a hit, and got a standing O, just crushing it at the audition ... we are sad to say that you are not going to be moving forward in the show.

Wait, what?

How could this be? Not only did I do everything they asked me to do, but I got the *best* audience reaction possible.

A phone call followed. "Eric, we are so sorry, but your story is not *interesting enough* to have you advance."

Then I remembered my friends' advice. You needed a story. You needed that hook to get people to root for you.

After a while, I thought about it, and I understood.

Because if you really look at who "Eric O'Shea" was to the producers of this show, my story was far too "average." I wasn't sick with cancer. I wasn't bullied as a child. I didn't have a disability. I wasn't young and hopeful. I wasn't a starving artist. Even Howie joked to me on stage, "Wow, I bet you *really* make a great living doing this, Mr. O'Shea."

To which I humbly said, "I do."

So to sum it up? Despite the standing ovation and wonderful praise, it was my "story" that wasn't interesting enough to have me advance in the show.

And as you can imagine, I was a little heartbroken for a while.

But then I realized something.

Something that would thrill me for the rest of my life.

Very simply, I did it. I followed through. I took all the doubts, hurdles, frustrations, and killer process—with one creative arm tied behind my back—and still wowed them to their feet.

And that is something I will hang my hat on for the rest of my life.

That the guy who makes a "great living" doing colleges, in a rather demanding and isolating market, came out of his comfort zone for a moment and took a chance to show Hollywood—and America—what he could do and, without sounding too corny, who Eric O'Shea really was.

I don't know which was more exciting, hearing the people cheering me on and the cars beeping "great job" at me as I walked back to the hotel, or seeing myself on that box we call a television—something that I have always dreamt about as a child.

And as far as the airing of my episode? No, they didn't air my actual act, and the editing was a bit odd. Though they did show me blowing a slow-motion kiss to the crowd after an obvious job well done, and that's more than enough for me.

Now, can you see my performance online at least? Anywhere?

I wish you could, but sadly no. And the explanation I got also makes perfect sense. If I ever got the footage of my standing O and put it all over social media to boost my resume, it would make the show look ridiculous for not choosing me. People would ask, "Hey, why the hell didn't they use this guy?

So I understand. And I am completely at peace about it. Honest.

And if you really think about it? How *could* you be upset? Sure, it would have been fun to do another two minutes. But it was an amazing, fast-paced, always-evolving, pinch-me-moment experience that was almost like some sort of Hollywood boot camp.

And in my heart, I came out on top, and that's all that matters in (here it is again for the umpteenth time) the bigger picture.

When I look back on my life, I can be proud that for one moment, I was one of the best things that show had ever seen.

Hey, no one ever said this business was fair. It doesn't owe you anything.

So hold on to that knowledge and cherish every single experience in this business like your life depends on it.

Because it does. All we have at the end are memories, so make them wonderful!

And always remember, if you are lucky enough to rest your head at night in peace, knowing you made a difference while being a wonderful person, honoring your true self, and affecting other people's lives for the better … wow.

It just might be as good as hearing that ever-desirable golden buzzer.

Actually, it's probably better than that.

So, go on out there, and get yours.

I'm rootin' for ya!

WHERE HAVE YOU GONE, JOE DIMAGGIO?

Back in the day, effort came before fame. To get monumental praise, you had to show that you'd put in a little hard work—some real blood, sweat, and tears—and gone through life with discipline and something of a moral compass.

Nowadays? The formula seems to have reversed with fame coming long before it ought to. Look around. Throw out one viral video of snorting cinnamon for two minutes or folding tube socks in a hot, barely-there bikini, and now you're a "star" with millions of hits on YouTube, a few morning-show appearances, and even some "celebrity" judging on reality TV.

The main ingredient in this minimal-effort formula? A big, desperate, heaping tablespoon of sex and shock value.

Aw crap, here come the critics again.

"Now just wait a minute, Eric! Before you go any further with your uptight arrogance and your hater vibes, could it be possible that you are—how can I say this?—just a little bit *jealous*?"

No, not at all.

This issue has nothing to do with how I *feel* and more to do with what actual *behavior* is taking place.

Sadly, the problem is twofold: (1) the extremely poor quality of "entertainment" that is being put out there and (2) the ever-so-dangerous ripple effect that follows after.

Thanks to the internet, a quick launch toward "success" is simply fool's gold—and not just for the "star," but for the country as a whole. We're literally baiting our youth with the false sense that short video clips provide a path to long-term success.

Consequently, some youth think they have a sort of insurance policy—that if becoming a teacher or a doctor doesn't work out, they can simply flash some abs or try some other pointless stunt to "make it," not realizing that this path is a dead end and a horrible waste of a precious mind and soul.

(Oh, and for the record, the bitter, middle-aged people who buy into that false philosophy look even more ridiculous.)

Now look, I am not trying to be a buzzkill here, as some of these frivolous stunts and quick look-at-me moments can sometimes be clever and provide a much-needed laugh.

But the reality is all too obvious. Too many people are simply hurting themselves and taking the cheap, easy way out, squashing genuine and productive talents—*beneficial* talents—that, with a little more effort, would not only improve those people, but our world as a whole.

And sorry to break it to ya, but this has become more than an annoying problem. It's one that needs *immediate attention*—the kind a doctor gives to a dying patient.

We need some shock paddles to save our flatlining society.

Just look around! History, geography, *basic knowledge of our country*—forgotten relics of the past. And don't disregard the erosion of our incredible ancestors' sacrifices, which are basically being spat upon because there is something "way cooler" to flaunt in our pathetic attempts to be noticed.

Oh yeah, I'd say it's a big problem. And no, I didn't forget about the more dangerous ripple effect that I alluded to earlier. Chew on this.

Hollywood—having such a huge influence on our society and how people define success—has pretty much figured out the magic formula.

That is, they can *always* churn out new people in low budget reality shows to get ratings, all while cleverly using ego, pleasure, and excess—despite the dangers of weakening a society—as simply "the way to go."

And just when you think you've then seen the worst, a new bottom is created, practically begging to be challenged.

Now—and I don't think I am being overly dramatic here—not only are we a society of pleasure-seeking, attention-seeking addicts, we are a society of full-fledged *junkies*.

Sadly, this lifestyle feels way too good to give up, and it's gonna take one hell of an intervention to get us back.

But the good news?

Change is coming. I can feel it. You can see it.

Finally, we are calling each other out to grow up a little bit and dig a hell of a lot deeper!

And yes, although there was really "nowhere to go but up," there certainly is a refreshing level of accountability taking place. Through some real self-awareness and effort, we have finally started going back in the right direction.

But let's keep working.

And in the meantime, perhaps YouTube some wholesome, family friendly, hilarious comedy videos from yours truly!

(Ugh. What a shameless plug! Meh, who cares. Read on!)

DOCTOR! DOCTOR! GIVE ME THE VIEWS!

I got a … bad caaase … of watchin' youuu!

Sorry, I got a little carried away. But when you are on day thirty-two of a global stay-at-home quarantine for the coronavirus, you can go a little stir-crazy.

(That's right, it only took a global pandemic for me to actually write this book.)

But speaking of the virus, I want to take a moment and share my experience with *viral* videos and what they do for a comedy career.

There is nothing more gratifying and exposure-boosting than having some viral videos make their way around the globe. And thankfully, I have had several.

But before I start, however, I want to give mad props to this little thing called "the internet." Yes, I'd like to think that my "talent" and "humor" has *something* to do with it, but I am not blind to the fact that, without the internet, my jokes would merely be confined to whoever came out that night to see me, not millions and millions of people.

I thank God every day that my comedy journey is happening during a time when we have the ability to reach anyone, anywhere, at any time.

And man, there are a lot of people out there! I can't stop pinching myself at all the views my videos keep racking up. From my Elmo bit to "Songs for Commercials" to my Dry Bar Comedy special, we are approaching over 25 *million* in total.

And I say that with *incredible humility*. Honest.

But don't get me wrong. Is it fun to count the number of hits and views in a society where the higher the number the "cooler" you are?

Of course it is.

But to a guy who has never tweeted (tweeting seems only good for two things: offending someone and then apologizing for it) and doesn't even have a fan page anywhere, it is very gratifying to have an additional outlet to do comedy besides stand-up and to know that you are still getting your name out there.

And speaking of getting your name out there, it is no mystery that your exposure can do wonders for your comedic opportunities!

And thankfully, because of the number of hits, I have gotten hundreds of bookings, auditions, and many of the cool pinch-me moments that I write about in this book. Top Hollywood people now know who I am, including—brace yourself for a cringy name drop coming in three, two, one—oh, just some little, no-name producer named *Steven Spielberg*.

Yep, and according to his many assistants, Mr. Spielberg loved my "Songs for Commercials" so much that he added a link to it *to the home screen of his laptop!*"

Seriously, pinch me.

This resulted in being flown out to Hollywood to audition for a Fox TV pilot. But afterward, I was told, "Although you were Steven's number one male choice, with so many male hosts already out there, we are going to give the job to a female."

Darn! So close!

(And before you ask, cross-dressing never crossed my mind, but I *know* I would look great in a dress. C'mon, with these legs?!)

But this is just one example of one of the many exciting moments that I have experienced from a viral video making the rounds.

However, as I get older, there is yet another aspect of viral videos that is important to address—and it really gets to the core of *why* we comics do what we do: to touch another person's life, for just one brief moment, to make them happy.

I cannot tell you how many people from all over the world write to me every day, telling me how much I make them laugh—or even better, how much they needed to laugh that day.

From fifteen-year-old kids wanting to be comics to retired grandparents looking for some company, I have received touching emails from people thanking me for making their day a little brighter.

One of my favorite emails came from a Saudi Arabian man in his twenties, and he told me he was trying comedy for the very first time. For good luck, he printed out a picture of me (with my name in Arabic) and kept it in his pocket on stage while performing—because I was his favorite comedian.

I was so touched! And according to him, his set went great (not that I had anything to do with it)!

It's moments like this that make viral videos so rewarding. And selfishly, this kind of feedback helps me feel good about what I do and why I do it. There is nothing like seeing chemistry between two strangers come to fruition.

Through comedy, two people can feel a rare, emotional bond across thousands of miles and, for one moment, smile together.

THE REVIEWS ARE IN!

One of the greatest gifts you can give a comic after a show is, of course, a nice compliment. No matter whether it is a quick "Hey, great job!" in the lobby of a theater or a single like on social media, I am always so thankful. But after doing my Dry Bar Comedy special, which again, now has clips that have been viewed over 20 million times around the world, I've actually been a little caught off guard by the responses I've received.

And yes, I'm also so glad they speak to me in English, or I'd be in deep trouble!

(Well, I am tired of getting scammed by these "royal princes" who keep asking me to send them money. I'm still waiting for six return checks! Sigh. I'll give it another week.)

Anyway, I just want to take a moment to share with you just a few emails from some wonderful people that really made my day. Hell, they made my year! Ah, who am I kidding? More like my *life*.

Here they are:

Hello from down under! (Australia, that is.) Just wanted to thank you for the laugh! I haven't belly laughed like that in forever. I now have to find my dog, 'cause it scared the crap outta him, and he is now hiding!

My thirteen-year-old daughter and I were proper creasing up last night watching you at the Dry Bar. Haven't had a laughter-inspired asthma attack in a while. Stomach muscle's sore but totally worth it!

(You gotta love "proper creasing up." So cute!)

Hey Mr. O'Shea! I'm from Malaysia and saw your video. It was epic!

Thank you for making me laugh. Even when I didn't think I could anymore. Forever a fan!

Oh my gosh! Just watched your Dry Bar Comedy special. I usually watch Dry Bar while I work out. It helps the time go by faster. Today I watched yours and almost fell off the elliptical, I was laughing so hard! I totally needed a forty-five-minute belly laugh, as I'm sure many people do during this time. Super awesomely funny! I am so grateful that you reminded me at how everyday life can be laughed at. Thank you, thank you, thank you!

Hi Eric. My name is Gage. I'm fifteen, and I just wanna say your comedy kills me. It is so incredible and funny. Your impression of misbehaving kids is spot on me when I was younger. You are so funny. Have a great rest of your day.

Hi Eric. I know you probably hear this all the time, but your comedy made me laugh out loud like I haven't in years! Thank you for seeing the humor in everyday life! Your wife is very lucky.

Welp, I'm gonna stop here for now—because (1) it appears that I now have to find a bride, and (2) any more of these reviews, and I could probably be accused of showboating. But again, I merely do so only because I am just so grateful to even *have the opportunity* to share some of these unexpected emails—*blessings*, rather—that not only touch my heart but have given *me* the chance to be the one chuckling out loud.

Yes, sometimes it's actually nice to be on the other side of a laugh.

FUN FACTS...
ABOUT THE AUTHOR!

I know, I know. The last chapter was *so* one sided. Everyone laid bare their souls to the world—everyone except me, that is.

Well that's not fair!

So, without any further ado, and in no particular order, here are some completely random fun facts about (*he enters into a Southern belle accent and fans himself*) lil' ol' maaay!!

Here we go!

Humble Beginnings

I was born at Yale New Haven Hospital on a Wednesday at about noon, September 16, 1970, weighing a whopping five pounds, fifteen and three-quarters ounces, just shy of a six-pound bag of potatoes.

As I was being born, the umbilical cord wrapped around my neck, choking me a bit. Although there is no proof I was deprived of oxygen, this may explain my unique ... disposition.

My second year of life was rough. I cracked my head open on the corner of a nightstand table, broke my collarbone, and, when I tried to eat a large piece of hot dog in my high chair, nearly choked to death (again) and turned blue. My mom stuck her fingers down my throat and got it out, piercing and grabbing it with her long fingernails.

I was also reading pretty well by the time I was two and a half—no Shakespeare, though. But I was just fascinated with the magnetic letters on my Fisher Price schoolhouse.

When I was five, I refused to go in the water all summer at our summer cottage on a lake. I swore a fish bit my toe, so I spent all three months just pushing the older kids off the dock. They felt bad for my *fishy* story, I think.

I once screamed at my brother who accidentally let go of a raft with me in it. Panicking as I drifted away at 0.00001 miles an hour, I pleaded, "George! What are you doing? You know I can't *oar*!" I couldn't row either.

I once caught a fish with a homemade fishing pole made from a stick from the woods, two feet of clear string, and a bare hook. No casting required. I just lowered the hook into the water and *bam*! An eight-inch bass!

I once cried in the first grade when I couldn't find my Catholic school uniform sweater, prompting the whole class to stop everything and look for it. They checked everywhere—desks, chairs, coat hooks, closets. Turns out I was wearing it. I'm not sure who was more clueless, me or the other twenty-nine kids and the teacher who didn't see it either.

I was always a shy yet observant kid. That ability to memorize every move, expression, and behavior of people worked great for imitating them.

I was a huge goodie two-shoes often sitting in the front of the class, the first seat on the bus, and always wanting to do the right thing. Why? Because I was taught that way. I was also one of only four people in my class to go all the way from kindergarten to eighth grade at my school.

At recess, I always pretended to be Roger Staubach and Danny White from the Dallas Cowboys, and in our neighborhood whiffle ball games, Dave Winfield.

I have been imitating people since third grade when I would portray Jack Tripper from the previous night's *Three's Company* episode for the kids at school. Ill-advised or not, I also imitated my classmates and teachers, both in grammar school and in high school.

Between St. Brendan's, Gramps, his diner, Hancock, New York, and the summer cottage, the 1970s was without a doubt the greatest time of my life.

I was an altar boy for seven years and enjoyed being raised Catholic. Although, if I'm ever being sworn under oath in court, I'm switching to atheism.

Them: "Do you swear to tell the truth, the whole truth, and nothing but the truth, so help you God?"

Me: "Who?"

Them: "God."

Me: (*Pausing with a subtle dismissive chuckle.*) "Um … yeah, sure."

I once saw a centerfold of a *Playboy* magazine. When I got out of the bathtub and dried off one night, I excitedly ran in the bedroom that I shared with my brother, jumped on my twin mattress completely naked, and threw my legs up over my head telling him, "This is what the girls do in those dirty magazines!"

Unbeknownst to me, my mother was standing in the doorway. Very upset, and with *huge* intimidating eyes, she said firmly, "Put. Some clothes on. Right. NOW!" I quickly did.

I took piano lessons for six years.

My high school was an all-boys college prep school, with jacket and tie and everything—very challenging. I went through an awkward chubby phase during those four years. I wasn't fat, but definitely the Three H's: husky, hairless, and hopeless.

During my freshman year in high school, I took a carpool, thirty-minute train ride, and two buses every morning and night. And because I was the smallest kid in the carpool, I was put in the hatchback trunk with all the book bags. I am very thankful no one rear-ended that car ...

When I was fourteen, I was on my second bus trip home by myself at night in the middle of winter. My book bag was ridiculously full, hanging heavily two feet off my back. When the bus moved sharply, I lost my balance and fell onto a lady, hitting her in the face with all my books. She pushed me hard and screamed, "Get off me!"

I worked some very random jobs growing up. Dishwasher and cashier at Gramps's diner, Dairy Queen server, summer camp counselor for kids with Down syndrome, and security guard walking the aisles of Walgreens looking out for shoplifters. I was so good as a security guard that they moved me to the night shift at a hospital where I would roam the dark halls at 3:00 a.m., checking for unlocked doors and being scared half to death by the silhouettes of elderly people sitting upright in their beds. Then I transferred to a less scary post: guarding a dangerous hole at a construction site in the middle of nowhere. For eight hours a day, I would pass the time by hitting rocks into the field with my whiffle ball bat or by throwing a toilet paper roll as high as I could. No, there was no bathroom. Anything for a paycheck.

I met Hulk Hogan, Andre the Giant, and many other World Wrestling Federation wrestlers in 1984 when my mom worked at the old New Haven Coliseum.

The Go-Go's and Flock of Seagulls were my first concert. At a different concert, my older brother, younger sister, and I stood in the front row, staring straight up, completely mesmerized at a young, new performer seductively laying on some speakers. She only had a few hits at the time: "Borderline," "Lucky Star," and "Like a Virgin."

My first car I drove around with regularity was a 1976 green Dodge Diplomat—the "Green Machine."

I once took my mom's boyfriend's humongous cherry-red Cadillac El Dorado convertible to show off at school while they were in Italy. On the way home, I only had one more hill to go, and as I drove up it, thanking God that nothing bad had happened, some guy made a left turn down the hill—right in front of me. The Cadillac did a full 360-degree circle, and somehow I avoided not only the idiot driver, but two parked cars. All I remember was sitting there shaking, both hands squeezing the steering wheel, as a neighbor opened his front door and yelled at me, "Hey! You almost hit my car!"

I don't take people's cars without asking anymore.

Unique Tastes and Taste Buds

Speaking of Italy, I don't like olives. I also don't like mustard, horseradish, wasabi, peanut butter, marshmallows, caramel, or blue cheese.

But I love hot peppers: jalapeños, habaneros, ghost peppers.

You probably have already figured this out, but I'll also put ketchup and BBQ sauce on anything: bread, veggies, meat, fish, soup, crackers, cereal—my finger. Give me an IV, and I'll be set.

Kit Kat is my favorite candy bar, and I'd take Sour Patch Kids over Hershey kisses—but not by much.

I've never had a full cup of coffee, and I haven't had a sip of soda in over thirty years.

Generally speaking, I like to be healthy. I love sushi, beef stew, grilled veggies, coconut water, Evian water, and fruit. To stay physically fit, I play tennis, shoot three-pointers, bowl, throw a Nerf, and swim. For my mind, I play chess, board games, poker, *Jeopardy!*, trivia, and word games like Scrabble.

I love numbers but absolutely hate Sudoku.

If I'm on vacation, I'll take a fancy pool over sand and the ocean. At nighttime, I'll take the opposite.

I *hate* dishes in the sink. All a sink is, is just another damn counter six inches lower with sides around it!

I am a huge minimalist. I don't like clutter, excess, or material nonsense. I can live with just the basics—and I'm not kidding. My wardrobe is like a cartoon character's, with nineteen identical outfits. Whenever I blow up from dynamite, I know I'll look good again in no time, no matter the hangar.

I donate tons of stuff or give things away just to get it the hell out of my house . . .

I will never ride on a motorcycle. I think they look cool, and I respect all who ride them, but they are far too dangerous for my taste. "But I ride a state-of-the-art Yamaha and have never been in an accident!" I hear you say. Well, I'm not worried about you and your flawless accident record. I'm worried about that eighty-eight-year-old driver who just ran a stoplight and broad-sided you while doing fifty-five, or the speeding teen texting who knocked you over and just broke every bone in your lower body.

Motorcycles are awesome, but the wonderful riders are *way* too exposed and vulnerable for my taste.

I also can't stand the insane, decibel-clubbing grinding of a Harley just idling there doing nothing. I'm sorry, but it gives me a killer headache! OK, I'm done being a wuss now (*he says as the leader of the Hell's Angels makes him hand in his leather chaps*).

My favorite color is blue. I love blue sneakers, blue shirts, and blue shorts. I'm like the Johnny Cash of wearing all blue.

My go-to alcoholic beverage is pinot grigio, and it only takes me two glasses to pass out. I'm a cheap date.

The best steak I ever had was in Storm Lake, Iowa, and the best burrito I ever had was in Nacogdoches, Texas.

I've been around.

No, not like that.

Putting Myself Out There

I was the first male waiter to ever work at Jimmy's Seafood Restaurant (established in 1925) in Hamden, Connecticut. I then got asked to do a voice-over ad for the restaurant, which aired all over KC101 FM.

It was really neat to drive down Whalley Avenue and hear my own voice blasting out of the car in traffic.

I lived in Milwaukee from 1988 to 1992, then from 1993 to 1996.

I majored in communications at Marquette University because I always wanted to be a sportscaster. My freshman year, I was coerced by a wonderful group of friends in my dorm to join them at Milwaukee County Stadium for the taping of "some baseball movie." With the director in a huge cherry picker, he yelled and pointed at two of us in our group, out of dozens of people, to be extras sitting in the bleachers. Now every time I see the movie *Major League*, I revel in those four seconds where my friend Liz and I are talking to each other, pretending to be frustrated Indians fans.

After doing tons of TV newscasts and play-by-plays of basketball games throughout college, a TV station was very impressed with my demo reel. Then, in my senior year, I dropped a huge bomb on my family. "I think I want to be a stand-up comedian," I said. I remember many professors and friends thinking I was crazy to want to drop broadcasting—what looked like a natural skill of mine—for stand-up comedy. I can understand that now.

I was once so broke—I'm talking no credit card, no cash, or even pennies in my Ford Escort ashtray— that I had to borrow $10 to pay for a big-ticket toll while driving on I-90 for seven hours to get to a $300 emcee gig. I pulled over at a rest stop an exit before and told a guy I lost my wallet and would pay him back if he just gave me his address. He said not to worry and just gave me the money anyway. When I finally arrived, I then begged the club owner to front me $50 for the weekend until I got paid. After thinking about it for a hot minute, he finally did.

I skipped class to go to Jeffrey Dahmer's court hearing across the street from my residence hall. He was in a bulletproof chamber for his protection. Afterward, my friend and I got a little gutsy and went to his actual apartment—which was covered with police tape and was where he brought his victims—quickly touched it, and ran away like two terrified little kids.

In 1992, that same friend and I went to a taping of *SNL* because his father was an old college roommate of the director. I was so excited to meet all the cast members, but the ones who really stood out were Mike Myers and Phil Hartman—two complete gentlemen. I wandered on stage during a skit rehearsal, and Phil Hartman thought I was in it. With an eyebrow raised, he said in his charming voice, "So, are you an extra?" I felt *sooo* cool. But what really took the cake, without a doubt, was the moment I got to shake the hand of legendary announcer Don Pardo. He was so unbelievably kind to me. And then, without even flinching, he took a deep breath and bellowed, "It's *Saturday Night Live!* Starring Eric O'Shea!"

And after every last goose bump popped—yes, it was official—I would die a happy man.

Feeling Sporty

I love watching the NFL, NBA, and MLB, but two games that I saw live and in person really stand out to me: the 2007 Super Bowl, in which the Giant's David Tyree somehow caught the football with his helmet, and Game Six of the 2009 World Series, when the Yankees won and jumped all over each other for the World Championship. And yes, while trotting on a horse after the game, Dave Winfield smiled and waved to me.

I had the honor of watching many athletes play live: Michael Jordan in 1991, Magic Johnson in 1990, Kobe Bryant in 2010, Joe Montana in 1984, and Derek Jeter and the entire Yankee dynasty numerous times. I even went to, and narrated on camera, Derek Jeter's last hit at Yankee Stadium—a base hit to right field with his classic inside-out swing to win the game.

Name any year, and I'll tell you not only who won in the NFL, NBA, MLB, and NCAA tournament, but also what happened and who made it happen. I know. It's a sickness.

In 1996, I was in a high-end mall in downtown Chicago, where I saw Dennis Rodman. I followed him into a store while he looked at some items in a glass display case. I mimicked everything he did. When he moved over to a new display, I moved over to a new display. Then I realized that he was looking at nail polish. So, yes, I had to pretend that I was looking at nail polish too. He then caught on and smiled as I quickly turned away. But knowing I was busted, I eventually smiled back and asked to shake his hand. He laughed and said sure, but the whole time I was simply in awe, thinking, "This is incredible. It's Dennis Rodman! I'll never wash this hand again." Then, thinking about it a bit more, I thought, "Actually, as cool and nice as he was, I probably should."

I once won a three-point contest at a Marquette ladies basketball halftime giveaway by making twenty-two of them in sixty seconds.

The prize was a free burger at Hardee's.

The Big Apple

On April 22, 1997, I moved to New York City, where I spent the next eighteen years of my life on the Upper West Side of Manhattan. My first apartment was on West 78th Street and Broadway. This little nugget was my pride and joy. It was a brownstone studio apartment with a private entrance, stucco walls, and fireplace, right on the street. My second apartment, however, was only 400 square feet in Harlem on the top of Central Park North. I shared this tiny, two-bedroom shoebox of a place with a wonderful gal from Haiti. I traveled a lot and saved tons of money.

NYC is the greatest city in the world.

On September 10, 2001, I took a taxi from my NYC apartment to LaGuardia and fell asleep on the terminal floor—which I *never* do! My Northwest flight was calling final boarding, and a lady woke me up to finally get on the plane. Without her, I would have missed the plane! I then did a school in Rapid City, South Dakota, that night for a crowd in a small ballroom and went to bed in a tiny hotel, as usual. I didn't own a cellphone then, and the landline rings in my room the next morning.

"Eric? Hi. So, here's what's going on. There are two planes that crashed into the World Trade Center. There is no more World Trade Center, and all the airports are closed. Is there anything we can do for you?"

I'm half-asleep and dazed. I turn on the old, boxy TV and find bad reception on every channel. Then I see fuzzy live shots of this world-changing moment. I wasn't sure what to think. I just felt shock and a pit in my stomach, like all of us. Funny how life stops. I was going to Mt. Rushmore for the second time, but instead I took a rental car all the way to Minneapolis. When the airports opened, I was on the third flight back to New York, which had only eleven people on board. Everyone was so quiet, and there was no assigned seating. Sit anywhere. We heard the pilot say somberly, "This is your captain. We will get you to NYC as safely as possible. Thanks."

A guy got up to use the bathroom, and you could hear everyone's heart racing. The fear was so raw. We landed, and the crew just yelled, "Go, go, go! Everybody, just keep going please!" On September 14, I played Wagner College on Staten Island, and while on a ferry, I filmed the smoke still rising, the wreckage still burning. I recorded all the missing-person flyers in the Village, candles all around, masses of people panicking. I have the footage in my dresser drawer, but have still never watched it. They say to never forget, so I won't. I will watch it someday. Rest in peace to all those in a better place.

(Thank you for reading that. It meant a lot for me to share that with you. Now back to the fun.)

I spent three New Year's Eves in Times Square. The first one was with my good friend Bob, when 1992 was turning 1993. We spent the night chatting up two French gals who didn't speak a word of English. My second NYC New Year's was December 1998, where I gazed down with a girlfriend at all the insanity from the gazillionth floor of the

Marriott Marquis. The third New Year's was a year later to celebrate the new millennium and cope with anxieties about Y2K, and it *definitely* was the most memorable.

There I stood with my two friends, bracing for a potential blackout, but with confetti in hand, amid the deafening screaming on 42nd Street. As the clock ticked down, people's voices reached their peak. "Five, four, three, two, one!"

Boom! No blackout, but absolute sheer pandemonium.

And as everyone was going crazy, jumping all over and kissing each other, there I stood, stoic, just staring at the extremely tall man next to me. All of my confetti landed in his gigantic afro. He seemed like a super nice guy, dancing and screaming, but he never noticed. Happy New Year!

In 1999, I met Jerry Seinfeld at a tiny newspaper stand on the Upper West Side, right outside my apartment. He had a baseball cap on, and I just stood there, not sure what to do. Just the two of us there, I nervously said, "Excuse me, Jerry? I am a stand-up comedian of six years, and forgive me, but it would be a shame not to shake your hand."

He responded with his quick wit. "Yeah, it would be bad luck, wouldn't it?" We shook hands, and for the record, I never thought that any man could ever have softer hands than me. As we gripped each other's palms, it was like squeezing Play-Doh. Weird but oddly comforting. (Well, what kind of manly hands did you expect from two fellow blue-collar steel workers?)

In 2002, I went to the actual Soup Nazi store from *Seinfeld* to see what the hype was all about. After I found all the militant customs and rules on how to order were 100 percent true, don't ask me why, but I got extremely brave and decided to start up a conversation with the angriest man alive himself. I told him that I was a comedian and that one of my influences was Jerry Seinfeld. Now I'm not sure if he thought I said "I *knew* Jerry Seinfeld," but for some reason his eyes got really big. He *smiled* at me, and then said that it was nice meeting me!

Oh my gosh! I thought. I'm *in* with this guy!

Well, it didn't last long. The very next day, when I went back for round two, he seemed a little bit grumpier and made zero eye contact with me. After I very meekly said "Um, hi. Remember me? The … um … comedian from yesterday?"

He lost his damn mind!

At the top of his lungs, in front of a packed lunch-hour line, he screamed, "Look! I don't know who you are! Now move to the left, please!"

Like a scolded child, with my head down and bag in hand, I took my soup and slowly made my way back to my apartment, completely baffled on what the hell just happened. Yet I savored two things: First, this was by far the most delicious, loaded, generously portioned, to-die-for seafood chowder I'd ever had! Second, well, at least he didn't scream "No soup for you!"

I once wore a black button-down shirt with a homemade priest collar to an audition in a Dan Aykroyd priest sitcom. I didn't get the role, but I looked so convincing that my driver actually said, "Thank you, Father. Have a good day!"

I once got as far as "testing" for a sitcom alongside Kyra Sedgwick. The director said I did great but was actually *too funny* and upstaged her. I didn't get the part.

On October 18, 1996, I was on a show called *NBC Friday Night Videos*. I remember the exact date because it was my brother's wedding rehearsal dinner. A bunch of us caught the airing at the restaurant bar.

In 2000, I got my first pilot for VH1 called *Couch Potato*, beating out over two-hundred male actors for the role. I auditioned with a very strong-willed, vampy gal, and our strategy going into the audition was to reverse the typical stereotypes of men and women when it came to wanting sex. While most couples auditioning did the usual guy-chasing-girl thing, what put us over the top was that *she* attacked *me* on the couch while I played "nervous and scared." (College prom night really helped me prepare for the role.) Filming the show at the Seaport with a full script, crew, and costumes was an amazing experience!

Comedic Influences

- Jerry Seinfeld, the master technician with his no-filler style.

- George Carlin and his all-around talent. Just incredible. Witty, brilliant, clever, funny, observational, thought-provoking, and *ballsy*.

- Bob Newhart, with his impeccable timing, misfortune, wit, and timeless skits. The quintessential "straight man."

- Jackie Gleason as Ralph Kramden. Grumpy, frustrated, lovable, misfortunate, high energy, and full of expressions. He was *so* easy to watch.

- Carroll O'Connor as Archie Bunker. See above. I can watch both he and Gleason all day.

- Bea Arthur as Dorothy on *Golden Girls*. Strong, with a rare mix of frustration and calm. Witty, with *insane* timing and delivery, and one of the only people who can literally do nothing except grimace with a slight pout and have the audience in tears. I learned so much from her!

I am not sure whether I have an actual "style" of comedy, but I certainly have borrowed bits and pieces from some of my comedic heroes, combined that inspiration with my own persona, and created my own unique comedic voice. Thankfully, that voice is very much authentic with who I am off the stage as well. Some of the common denominators of my comedic voice include observation, self-deprecation, eye-roll levels of feigned frustration, and (from what I'm told) extreme likability. (Aw!)

I've found myself falling in love with an exciting, "one-two-punch combination" when doing my routine: observing something that the crowd can relate *with*, then taking the bullet for the team and being the guy who the crowd gets to laugh *at*! So in essence, my style is about using two psychological strategies simultaneously to create a really fun, hard-hitting show that engages crowds—and their funny bones—on multiple levels.

Now, I am not implying that I originated this style of comedy or putting myself in the same category as my legendary comedic influences, but this style works so well for me, in part, because it aligns so well with who I am and how I enjoy making people laugh. I am just so very grateful to be able to dissect, understand, appreciate, and cultivate a style of comedy that not only comes to me quite naturally but also brings so much joy to the world.

Wow, That Was Random!

I love to learn about real estate and the housing market, as it has become a hobby of mine. I own several properties in both Austin, Texas, and Scottsdale, Arizona, both places I call home.

I love my bedroom in Scottsdale where I get so much done. Sleep, work, relaxing, and lots and lots of writing—including this book!

But I *hate* reading. I think I've only read three novels in my lifetime, and only because I was forced to in school. I have never read Shakespeare and have no desire to. My reading comprehension absolutely sucks. Always has. I also can't remember anything I just read. Remember those first-grade questions?

"Jack ate an apple." Who ate the apple?

    A. *Tom*

    B. *Jack*

    C. *Brian*

    D. *Phil*

Nine times out of ten, I'd put Phil. Freakin' ridiculous. But even though I am not book smart, I have a decent knowledge of facts and trivia.

I am absolutely terrified of heights, needles, and jail. Needless to say, if I was ever in a prison built on the edge of a cliff, I would cry every night.

I'm not good with hospital stuff and faint at the sight of blood. If there was an emergency, I'd be a *fourth* responder.

I still don't like to hang my feet off the edge of the mattress just in case that monster grabs ahold of my ankle and pulls me under the bed.

I absolutely love and am fascinated with the paranormal and UFOs, and it is just a matter of time until both reveal themselves more frequently because *of course* they exist. More on that later.

I once headlined the Mohegan Sun in Connecticut. They didn't have a dressing room ready for me, so they knocked on another dressing room door to make sure that it was available. No one answered, but inside were the coolest bedazzled sport coats, a freshly bitten sandwich, and a carbonated soda still fizzing. Wow, I must have just missed whomever it was.

It was Burt Reynolds.

Early in my career, I once performed at a county fair on a muddy field in rural Wisconsin. There might have been fifty people sitting in a field on lawn chairs, with Igloo coolers right beside them. The organizer told me to go on to the main stage, tell a quick joke, and tell the small crowd that I would be over at the comedy tent in thirty minutes. Unbeknownst to me, there was a very pretty and talented gal stage left completely cracking up at the one joke I told. As I then walked over to my spot, my friend said, "Wow, do you know who was laughing at your joke a second ago?"

"No," I said. "Who?"

It was Faith Hill.

Yes, I could have been her husband, Eric Hill. Sigh. The one that got away.

Anyway, back to reality.

I've never bought a new car. Although I did buy a 1998 BMW silver convertible in excellent condition with only 83,000 miles for $9,500 and used to own a fun moped that I rode on a desolate lake road.

I love groups like Journey, Bon Jovi, Chicago, Hall and Oates, Heart, and Huey Lewis and the News. There's also a special place in my heart for the one-hit wonders of the '80s, especially the cheesy power ballads.

And I have no problem singing them!

I *love* to sing, probably just as much as doing comedy—sometimes more. My go-to karaoke songs are "Wanted Dead or Alive" or Sinatra's "My Way," especially to serenade a packed house.

If you give me a blank United States map, I could draw you *every* interstate, even the new ones, coast to coast. I once did a radio show in LA for charity where listeners would call in trying to stump me. I got some wrong on purpose so that I'd have to donate some toys to kids. Aw!

I still have my Ellie the Elephant stuffed animal, who is still going strong from my days as an infant. He's still my pal. I want to be cremated with him some day and have some of our ashes tossed off the Empire State Building, my favorite building in the world.

I am a very quiet sleeper, and I have been told I twitch a bit. I make up for lost sleep with naps (when I can).

I only dated one gal in Austin, so no, all my exes are not from Texas.

I'll reluctantly say it again, if you didn't catch it the first time. My first date in high school was my senior prom, and I lost my virginity at twenty years old at my *college* senior prom.

Apparently, I have a thing for proms.

I've never kept a journal—and *why the hell would anyone?!* Think about the concept. Hmm, let's see. Let me write down all my most private and intimate thoughts in a book that someone will eventually find. Then they'll know that I have a secret fetish of making love in a hammock with a bilingual amputee. C'mon, man. You're just *asking* for trouble.

I am horrible at anything electronic or technological. I don't fix things either, but that's more of a mafia thing. I always "know a guy" who can do it for a "double sawbuck."

I hate lifting heavy objects. I'm the type that if there were four huge guys moving a grand piano into a house, I'd be the one who holds the screen door open. Then I would stand around with the rest of them after, all macho, looking at it, pretending to pant and sweat.

I don't know how to tie shoes the normal way. I still do the bunny ears. I make two hoops, cross them over, fold one through, and pull down. (Shut up, because they never come untied.)

I can be kinda selfish. Like, I would pretend I was in the military just to be one of the first ones to board my flight first.

Overhead Announcement: "We now welcome all military personnel to board!"

Skeptical Gate Agent: "Um, excuse me, sir. Where *exactly* did you serve?"

Me: "Um, Dairy Queen?"

(*Embarrassed, walks back to zone 9.*)

I never married, and not because I am against it or because I am afraid of commitment. I have had some amazing, wonderful girlfriends who taught me a lot. And while I have nothing bad to say about them—I was honored to have had that time with them—the relationships just simply ran their course. And, to be fair, I was also dedicated and devoted to a wonderful career that kept me moving around. So I thank those women, so much, for not only being a part of my journey, but also helping me grow. I hope they feel the same way. But as I now slow down and stick around, I would feel so blessed to grow old with a woman where the chemistry was undeniable and the respect even greater! (Of course, some fun romantic nights wouldn't hurt either, especially ones with lots of laughs, naps, and fun trips abroad!)

And if I ever have a baby girl? I will choose the name that I picked out at age seventeen—Sydney—and she would be a daddy's girl.

Top Priority

But for now, my family is my world.

My mom is my best friend, and she was simply born to love. As a mother, she sacrificed for the entire family with a positive energy and spirit like no other, instilling guts, wisdom, and street smarts for her children to ensure they thrived in this world. She is my biggest fan, as I am hers. Love ya, "Ma!"

I love my "baby" sister to the nth degree. She is a fantastic nurse and mama, and her attention to detail is second to none. It shows in all she does. I will always protect her, just as I did from day one when I rocked her in that old, dark baby carriage every morning before I went off to kindergarten. She will always be my baby sis.

I love my older brother, the most decent person I ever met. A gentle giant at 6 foot 4 and 280 pounds, he would do absolutely anything for anyone, even hold up a refrigerator for two minutes, shaking and kindly smiling at you, just so you could get your nickel that rolled under there.

As stated in an earlier chapter, my grandpa was my main male role model. He taught me how to drive, shave, work hard—and then work hard some more—and do things with character, accuracy, passion, and fun. I miss him every day, but he is always smiling in my heart.

I cherish my extended family in Hancock, New York (and those not here anymore), for being a part of who I am. They are that constant heartbeat of my youth from a more innocent era, and wherever they are will *always* be a place to call home.

My nephew is an amazing young man that I love so much and am so proud of. His skills and kindness have been a joy to watch over the years. I would do anything for him, even though he kills me at chess!

My two nieces, or "Unc's Girls," are two people that I would also simply die for. They are the most precious, polite, talented, awe-inspiring young ladies that I could ever imagine. I don't know how I got so lucky. I will *always* be there for them—for any problem, any celebration, and everything in between.

And even when I can't visit, they know that Uncle Eric "always comes back!"

Finally, I have never been happier in my life than I am right now, and although you hear that word—"happiness"—being thrown around a lot, I will put it this way. How happy am I on a scale of one to ten? Forty-nine. I just can't explain it, but I will try. In this past year, something within me just feels like the most wonderful new plateau of all plateaus. Yes, I have been happy before, excited about various projects and thrilled with the outcomes, but there is just some sort of a proud maturity that I feel—a willingness to be vulnerable and let go of all the "silly stuff" by sharing my journey with 100 percent authenticity. By writing this book and revealing my honest, loving quest, I hope to help others experience the same wonderful existence that God has blessed me with.

And I sincerely hope I have with this particular chapter.

Welp, that's about it. That's me in a nutshell.

I'm sure I forgot a few things, but if you have any questions, please don't hesitate to ask.

But if I do decline to answer, don't get upset.

Well, c'mon. A guy has to have *some* secrets!

(*Cocky wink. Starts to write secrets in journal like an idiot.*)

MY PET NAMED PEEVE

I have a lot of pet peeves, and they all scamper around my mind, driving me crazy.

I need some mental leashes and obedience classes to reign them in.

Because here's the truth: I'm human, and like every other human there are just some things that *really* get on my nerves.

So why don't we just have some fun here? Let's dig in and see whether our things-that-drive-me-crazy lists line up.

And we're off!

Actions Speak Louder Than Words

Well, they do—kinda. Don't get me wrong, I totally agree that you must back up what you say, especially in a relationship. I get it, 100 percent. But please make no mistake. Words are just as important. Words are powerful. How so? Just ask the child whose wealthy father "shows" his affection by buying expensive gifts to justify his absence but never says "I love you."

And it's not just any words, but the *right* words that matter. When you mess up and hurt someone's feelings, merely saying "Well, I apologize" can ring hollow. Here the gesture of apologizing is more the focus than the actual feeling behind it. Using words that communicate that feeling are most important. That's why a simple "I'm sorry"—where the focus is on that deep feeling originating from inside you—can be more meaningful. It shows sincerity in your vulnerability and shows that you hold yourself accountable. For those of you rolling your eyes right now,

I get it. I know this slight adjustment won't ever stop World War III. But I really believe that, on a larger scale, a slight tweak like this one can quickly transform some very fixable bad habits and really make one heck of a difference in mending our most precious relationships.

Oh, and if you still think I'm being overdramatic here and still think switching to "I'm sorry" isn't all that important, that's OK. No problem. But the next time someone accidentally shoots you in the foot and calmly responds with the oh-so-lovely words, "Oops, m' bad," don't blame me when I just shrug my shoulders, smile, and walk away.

Hiking

I'm gonna take a lot of crap for this, but I really don't care—not one stinkin' bit. I'm just going to say it loud and clear.

Nothing good has ever come from hiking!

First of all, when in the hell did we suddenly take our ancestors' only grueling way of transportation to get over a mountain and mock them by turning it into a look-at-me-in-my-brand-new-yoga-outfit-posing-at-the-top-with-one-foot-flattened-up-on-my-inner-leg-praying-namaste kind of joke?

Sorry, it's ridiculous, and it has to stop.

Wait, now I will say that I have no problem with those of you who consistently live that lifestyle and who absolutely love nature and respect the power and majestic beauty of the earth. I have no problem with you. None. But for the majority (and you know who they are!) who turned hiking into this selfie-portfolio exercise, please get the hell away from me. (*Fake anger, but also not really.*) You should be ashamed of yourself and lack of individuality.

Oh, and for the record, if you ever get stranded on your climb (with your minimal experience and cocky attitude) and call for help? Sorry, Davy Crockett. You're on your own. Nope, no more rescue helicopters or nightly search parties eating up my tax dollars because you weren't prepared or humble enough to put the power of the earth over your self-centered attempt to impress social media. Nope. Now go and sleep on your new eighty-dollar North Face sweatshirt for the night, or better yet, keep yourself from completely panicking by counting the steps on your new Apple Watch.

The two of you were made for each other.

Texting and Driving

I say this one not only because it's obviously selfish and reckless to risk accidentally killing someone and ruining their loved one's lives forever just to answer the all-too-important question of "Yo, where ya at?"—but also because there are so many idiots who glance down at their phones to simply read a text!

And I love when they deny it.

I once pulled alongside a car at a red light and yelled at a guy to get off his damn phone! He got really nervous and said, "Um, I wasn't on my phone."

Disgusted, I replied, "Yeah, I know. You were just looking down and smiling at your crotch for five seconds for no reason!"

I angrily waved at my crotch and sped away, yelling "Oh, hello, Pen-is!" (pronounced *pen*, like a ball-point pen, and *iss*, like "kiss").

Wake up!

Line Lurkers

And speaking of waking up . . .

How about people standing in line not paying attention that they're next?! OMG, somebody cattle-prod me in the head.

You've been there! There are six people in line, it's hot, you're tired, and their only job was to keep their eyes on an open register—and they can't even do that!

Freakin' daydreaming twit!

Well, it sucks!

C'mon! I'm saying, "Guh-head." The guy behind me is saying, "Guh-head." The cashier is frantically waving, "Um, sir?" like some desperate castoff on a desert island signaling for help.

Sorry, but there should be a new rule! You just lost your spot and have to go back to the end of the line.

And walk backwards.

With your finger up your nose.

Balancing a Twix bar on your head.

Saying, "I shouldn't be allowed out in public" every ten seconds.

Maybe that will help you remember next time.

People Who Arrogantly Overuse Earplugs

Look, I get it. It's a loud flight, or there's construction outside your window while you're trying to sleep. But you know those people who make that snotty face and quickly shove in earplugs for even just the most basic sounds?

Holy crapola, it's annoying—not to mention, an insult to deaf people!

"Oh, I'm sorry. Too much *noise* for ya? *Hearing too much?*"

Nice, way to go demeaning the audibly challenged.

Too Many Choices!

Is it me, or are there now like nineteen different varieties of *one* product! Holy crap, I once got back from CVS and swallowed a probiotic—*for vaginal support*. And the scary thing is, I think something is working! Unbelievable.

Greedy CEOs Who Are Never Satisfied with Their Net Worth

Hey, scum of the earth. So you are *still* trying to accumulate wealth. Seriously? You are worth $49 billion dollars! To put that in perspective, do you realize that even if you misplaced $48 billion—and we're talkin' gone, like "Oh my God, I lost it!"—you'd still have *a billion dollars!*

(Now give me some!)

Bland Birthday Cards

So it's your special day—your birthday. You've waited a whole 365 days for this moment to come around again. And it's finally here. And all that person got you was one of those generic, vanilla, zero-thought-put-into-it, stupid, rhyming birthday cards.

Oh, you've seen them!

You're so great for all the things you do ...
Blah, blah, blah for all the whole year through ...
Blah, blah, blah in such a special way ...
Blah, blah, blah, so have a happy day!

Nice.

Why don't you just wake me up and punch me in the face.

Awful Knee Braces

And who in the hell designed those stupid knee braces with the huge hole in the middle—where your entire kneecap is still exposed? Yay, perfect! Not only did I bang my kneecap on the front of the bookshelf, but now it is getting extremely sunburned.

(*Rips off brace and angrily slams it in the trash.*)

Ridiculous Facebook Chain-Letter Games

Look. I'm already stressed out and having a bad day. Wanna take the last ounce of my sanity and enthusiastically challenge me with this waste of time?

Hell, I can't even figure them out!

Hey friend! Take the first letter in your last name, multiply it by two, divide it by a ham sandwich, punch a door, take a piss, and subtract your sister's ass.

No. No, I won't do that. For the love of God, please leave me alone!

Rearview Mirror Trickery

To all the hot girls in the car in front of me who constantly lean in to check their teeth in their rearview mirror, please stop it.

Once again, I thought you were smiling at me. And you weren't.

(*Eye roll.*) Back to the single life.

"Hey, Could You Do Me a Solid?"

I'm sorry, but this just sounds like that they are asking me to take a dump. It's not only disgusting but makes me extremely uncomfortable.

And to make it worse?

It's usually shouted very loudly and with enthusiasm.

"Hey, dude! Can you do me a solid?"

Sigh. "Only if I can flush right away."

(But then again, it's probably a lot better than being asked to "go diarrhea"—better known as the ol' porcelain paintball game.)

"Don't Bend over to Pick up the Soap!"

To the guy who first said this, I really hate you. Now every time the soap slips around in the shower, I'm absolutely terrified that some huge guy named Bubba is about to officially "make me his bride."

I don't even pick it up. No way. And to date, there are currently forty-nine bars of soap sitting in the bottom of my bathtub.

Saying Goodbye—Again

This is for those "lovely" times when you are in a grocery store and run into an old friend that you haven't seen in years.

You know the drill. You get super excited, eye each other up and down, let out a big "Wow, it's been forever," ask about family members, congratulate them or give out condolences as is appropriate, and then end by practically screaming, "This has been great. We'll have to grab coffee sometime."

After a long, dramatic wave goodbye, you then *immediately see them again the next aisle over.*

You know that discomfort? The horror?

And then you actually make it even worse, by quickly turning away toward the very first shelf you see, awkwardly smiling and avoiding them, pretending to seriously examine a can of kidney beans that you never intended to buy.

Yes, very smooth.

Sigh. I'm never shopping for anything again.

"Speak Up!"

I hate when the cell phone reception suddenly goes bad, and the person on the other end *blames you for it!* There you are, in the middle of complimenting them on something, and they just cut you off screaming, "Heelllooo! I can't hear you! What are you doing?! Where are youuuuu?!"

Sigh. Oh, I'm sorry. I just decided to mix it up and hide between the mattresses for fun while talking to you.

Asshole.

"Undereducated" and "Overeducated"

Finally, back to a more serious comment. I like to think that I have a decent amount of knowledge, but I *definitely* am no genius. And for me, that's exactly what I like in a person. They reside in the middle ground between knowing and not knowing, have passions for some topics, but always keep open room to grow. So when it comes to the two types of people that drive me crazy, they are usually found at both ends of the spectrum.

Now, I won't call the first one dumb or stupid as there are many cultural, genetic, and environmental factors that play a huge role in education. Sometimes their "smarts" are not their fault. But it is extremely frustrating when people with little to no experience on a topic insecurely label or categorize certain people or ideas because of their lack of exposure. Sadly, such an outlook diminishes the tolerance and respect that every human being deserves.

The second type of person that gets on my nerves, however, is even more annoying. We will simply call them the know-it-alls. You've met them before, and aren't they a freakin' delight. These are the people who, for some reason—be it insecurity or some sort of superiority complex—need to constantly preach how you are doing something either wrong or not well enough. That's right, they usually waltz on to the scene with several master's degrees or a lot of book knowledge, and they love to tell you not only everything they know, but more importantly, everything you don't. Now, I am all for educated people with a purpose, but it's that insufferable, condescending attitude and "talking down" that *really* pisses me off.

And if that's not enough, when they do spew their "facts," I swear to God, sometimes I think they're actually making crap up! Well, excuse me! Now my blinking is actually creating a wind current that is adding to the destruction of the ozone layer and causing birds' flight patterns to be blown off course?!

Perfect. Got it.

Look, bottom line, it's not just what they are saying, but it's how awful they make us feel—that our efforts as decent, caring, well balanced, educated people always fall short. And in their egotistical attempts to passive-aggressively smirk and give us just that "one more thing to chew on," we feel not only extremely underappreciated, but undervalued as a contributing member of society.

And for that, and in the face of their all-important academic achievements, their final grade as a human being is an F.

OK, I'm done for now.

And in my effort to lightly mix humor and venting, I can actually hear some of you asking, "Wow, where in the heck did *this* side of Eric O'Shea come from? He seems like the coolest, hippest, thing goin' that you'd want to make part of your life!

(*Three years later.*)

Has Eric O'Shea been a part of your life? You may be entitled to compensation. Call the Law offices at …

(*Chuckling.*) I'm kidding. Don't worry. Everything I said came from a good place—a place of hope for all of us!

And on that note, I gotta go. I got so worked up I could *really* use a shower!

(*Steps around bars of soap and nervously turns the water on.*)

NYC AND ME

OK, I survived. I'm all dried off and back in my footsie pajamas.

Now I want to (briefly) set the jokes aside and give you some thoughts on my values as a person, specifically as they relate to my comedy career and the path I chose.

What follows is just an opinion coming from an authentic heart, with lots of positive energy and *tons* of reflection. Nothing that I say is meant to be demeaning, judgmental, or negative, and it is definitely not written with a broad brush to put people in boxes. I merely love discussion, thought-provoking topics, and the chance to inspire—again, my purpose for this book.

So, let's talk about New York City.

When it comes to being a comedian, most people say NYC is not a place to get good at. It is a place to *already* be good at it. Why? Because NYC is the most "character-building" city in the world. Oh, it will test you.

Thankfully, I had a lot of history there already.

My grandparents and parents are from Park Slope in Brooklyn, and I spent eighteen exciting years on the Upper West Side. I was also lucky enough to have a good friend in the fashion business who opened up my world to the huge downtown scene—glamorous celebrities, swanky hotel bars, and limitless adventure.

And I would *never* trade that experience for anything. I really had a ball.

But keep in mind, although I've had some amazing pinch-me moments in the city—some that I actually can't repeat here (*wink*)—when it came to my career, I always knew that my market was colleges, not clubs. Oh sure, I occasionally did a club set here and there, but it never really appealed.

And for the longest time, it used to really bother me that it didn't—especially after coming back from a hell run of eleven cities in thirteen days. For those keeping score at home, that's eleven one-way flights in airports all across the country, eleven rental cars, eleven hour-long shows by yourself, and being "on"—over thirteen days.

That's almost half a month of being away.

When I came home, hell yes, I was tired. Over time, though, I discovered I was really most excited about getting back to a simpler way of living. After a grueling tour, the last thing that I wanted to do was bounce around clubs for twenty-dollar sets late at night and hear myself talk again. (After two weeks of shows, I was sick of my own voice!)

What I really looked forward to were the "normal" things that people got to do every day. Maybe I'd treat myself at my favorite sushi place for a nice quiet dinner or, dare I say, socialize a bit and go on an actual date.

This is what was really important to me. This is what really mattered.

This revelation did not come as quickly as I would have liked either. I remember just sitting on my brownstone stoop, drinking a beer outside my little basement studio apartment, watching all the comics across the street at Stand-Up Live all huddled up, exchanging bits, and scarfing down pizza slices while waiting patiently for their spots. What in the hell is wrong with me? I thought to myself. Shouldn't I be over there honing some new jokes?

But then I'd remind myself that I just did three new jokes on tour, and they all went great.

Of course, that wasn't the end of it. Those taunting thoughts would continue.

Well, shouldn't you be over there *anyway* and be a part of the unique NYC comedy scene, rubbin' elbows with everyone?

But over time, I became even more sure of myself: Wow! No! I don't even really want to! It just doesn't move me the way that it does for other comics.

I went through that scenario a couple of times a year, and it really challenged me to think hard about my career path. But then it dawned on me. No matter how hard I tried to "fit in" to the city scene—and I tried many times at many different venues—*I just simply didn't have the passion to take that comedy route.*

And that is OK.

As I look back, I see how important *balance* was to me in my life, like doing *some* comedy on the road but also being there for my amazing family. Doting on my cute nieces and nephew showed me what was most important in my life: *reveling in the pure essence of being content.*

Ah yes, contentment—a horrible word in this business of never-ending possibilities where you are always perhaps missing out on something "greater."

But I was happy. So happy.

And so, after doing a gazillion colleges and making a very good living—one that I had never experienced growing up—I found myself loving the little things and rejoicing in my growth as a *complete* person. I'd found the right fit for me, and I've cherished it for twenty-seven years and counting.

So, yes, it's true. I never once tried for a TV late-night spot, prioritized doing tons of auditions, or aimed to become a Hollywood comedian. None of that sang to my soul. In some ways, where I ended up was very different than what I conceived of starting out, but it was where *I* was meant to be.

I have the utmost respect for those who chose to follow the other route, but I have found my path, and I no longer look back.

By focusing on the college market, I have the freedom to live the life I want off the stage. And to get on the stage, I don't feel like I have to compromise who I am. I am *very* big on character and morality, and I always have been. It is just ingrained in who I am. And although I am *far* from perfect, the time I've spent on Hollywood platforms revealed many aspects of the business that I don't have the patience for: the not-so-nice people, the crazy lifestyle, the quick highs, the dark lows that are so commonplace, the huge financial burdens of time between projects, the addictions, the temptations ...

No, I just never found that way very healthy. To live the life I sought, I had to look past the glitzy rainbows and roses, stay true to myself, and acknowledge that the heart wants what the heart wants.

As I've tried to live this sort of intentional life, I've also paid close attention to how the world, particularly NYC, has been changing around me. The more I looked, the more concerned and disappointed I became with the economics driving "the greatest city in the world," for it was clear to me that the city was losing some of the magnificent charm of smaller mom-and-pop businesses that made NYC so unique and special.

I can't tell you how many times I've revisited my old block and found that the "golden nuggets" that made the area have disappeared. It seems to happen in every area of the city, it seems. Every return trip, I find a restaurant here, a bar there, a small store, and *famous neighborhood landmarks* completely gone—replaced by huge multimillion-dollar condos, banks, pharmacies, and corporate chains.

Oh yes, exactly more of what this city needed. Sigh.

To me, NYC is now a land of the "haves" and the "have-nots," with no middle ground or middle class. And although NYC is one of many cities striving to keep up with the times, I never thought such change would so drastically affect it—my favorite place in the world.

Sadly, when I saw my studio apartment—located in the "coolest nook" of variety, culture, and tradition—go from $1,000 per month in 1997 to a whopping $1,950 per month, making it a "bargain" in what was quickly becoming a generic, corporate area catered to the wealthy, I had a difficult decision to make.

With all that was memorable gone, it was simply time to go.

But I guess that's what makes memories so wonderful. You get to hold on to the beauty of places and experiences that are over and done with, slip them into the back pocket of your mind, and pull them out again whenever you want.

Yes, those eighteen years in NYC were some of the best times in my adult life. And although I don't necessarily have the desire to live there anymore, I will *always* cherish going back.

Without a doubt, after all the lessons I learned during my time there, this self-proclaimed New Yorker knows that city will *always* be home.

(Oh, by the way, I forgot to say that I also hate snow, rats, overcrowding, and the smell of pee, so don't feel *too* sorry for me in sunny Arizona. *Wink*.)

FEELING WEAK?
YOUR DAILY MULTIVITAMIN

When you are immersed in something as physically taxing and mentally draining as comedy—with both the travel and anxiety about where your next paycheck will come from—it is still important to have the *right attitude* and *balance*.

What does this mean? It begins with being able to see yourself as one part of a larger world—that bigger picture.

Sometimes we don't remember to take a much-needed moment to step outside of ourselves. Without that, some small concern—and, of course, bigger ones as well—can dominate our lives. Suddenly that isolated problem becomes the only important thing going on in the world. When we let out problems rule us in this way, each problem becomes the latest newspaper headline of our lives, written on the front page for all to see.

But here is what we fail to consider when we adopt this mindset.

We forget about all the millions of people that lived before us and faced similar problems. We forget about the millions of people that will someday experience the same problem fifty years from now. We naively think that today is the only day that has ever existed. We then magnify these problems with stress, anger, tears, and low self-esteem, and even more sadly, we become oblivious to the special people in our lives.

I was as guilty of this as anyone.

But one day, I had a long talk with myself, and thankfully, I realized this: the world doesn't stop for our problems, but neither does the *beauty* of the world because of them! There is always something beautiful and life changing waiting for us.

So here's my advice. Go pick up a good book. Try a new hobby. Take a risk. Don't be afraid to fail. Trust your instincts. Listen to your heart. Honor history and what came before you, and think about what you can do to honor this earth before you leave it.

Yes, I know, that problem is still there, and it may be very real and somewhat serious. But you don't have to be a slave to it and miss out on a world of opportunity, blessings, and wonder.

Ultimately, I want you to see your challenge for what it is: a short story on the *back* page of your life.

Because every waking moment, you get to choose which headlines get front-page placement.

Your bigger news headline is born from attitude.

Your bigger news headline is born from balance.

No matter the difficulty, when you are in charge of a positive, long-term outlook, you are no longer a slave to life's temporary grief.

Having a balanced perspective and realizing that there was, is, and always will be something greater than you (and your problem) means the life you lead will always be far more rewarding.

So whether you nervously pick up a pen tonight to write a new joke or confront wholeheartedly a situation that dominates your life, I ask you to rewire your brain and take that challenge for what it is—*a new wonderful opportunity to learn, grow, and appreciate the bigger picture.*

And while you are addressing that dilemma, you will see that those other precious moments in life never left and were always right there, just waiting for you to rejoice in them!

Yes, attitude and balance. The secret recipe for a wonderful existence.

THE THREE THINGS FOR A REWARDING LIFE

OK, now to dig even deeper. (But don't worry, this will all be crystal clear for you and where the good stuff is!)

With all the stress we encounter and all the information we process every day, it's easy to inadvertently fill our minds with self-doubt, anxiety, and confusion about what our purpose is. Although I am not certified as a medical "anything," after stumbling on some of these mental hurdles myself, I have discovered ways to avoid such problems and live with confidence both in myself and in my purpose.

The first part of this is fully embracing the attitude of just letting life happen; that is, allowing life to organically move forward as it will (a basic concept) and accepting it.

Now I will share with you what I consider the three key things you can do to have a rewarding life.

And please note that I did not say "successful," which is a societal term. "Rewarding" is much more personal, and that difference is important.

Trust Yourself

You know what you really want to do—so just do it! Your self-confidence is your biggest weapon in this life, and I urge you to become your own best friend. You'll have to make some very important decisions along the way, and only you can decide which way to go. It's OK if you don't have all the answers right away. That is what discovery is all about. But you have to trust that your judgment and feelings are steering you in the right direction.

You've probably also heard one of my favorite sayings before: "Get comfortable being uncomfortable."

That nervous feeling you get in the pit of your stomach is actually a good thing, and taking note of when it occurs is key to trusting yourself. When something is both exciting and uncomfortable, you gain wonderful knowledge of who you are and what you want much faster.

If you truly listen to your heart, it will *never* let you down. Trusting yourself is the greatest gift that you will ever give to yourself.

No matter what happens in life, no matter what problems arise, minor or major, you can count on yourself to see you through.

Choose Joy, Not Happiness

How do you find happiness? Sadly, you can't. Happiness can never fully be attained.

Well, let me ask you something.

Have you noticed that every time you work your tail off to achieve something, there is always something else dangling in front of you? It teases, appearing before you as if to say, "Great, you just got that done, but now you have to do this to really be happy."

Like, you just passed that test, but you still have to graduate college to be happy. Then you graduate college and find you need to get a job to really be happy. Then you need to get married and have kids and make lots of money. Add into that the need to get well known and have millions of followers on social media—and the "needs" keep piling up.

It's an unattainable and very harmful vicious cycle.

And don't get me wrong. Although goals are wonderful to have, the anxiety and stress we put on our minds and hearts to keep wanting more and more in order to fully be satisfied and "fulfilled," I believe, is fool's gold.

Happiness, described this way, is results oriented.

Joy, however, is a different story. (Here you can start to smile.)

Joy is not about results. It is a personal feeling that comes from within. It comes from you, not what you achieve.

Let me ask you this: Is it so hard to wake up every morning and just be joyful? I'm not saying that life doesn't test you, but is it so difficult just to wake up joyful? Every morning, when I put my feet on the floor, I pray and give thanks for the many choices I can make in life. I give thanks because I can walk, see, and hear! I can go left, I can go right. I have people who love me and whom I love so much in return!

Please don't forget the basics! The basics are blessings, and you should count them every day. Do you realize how lucky you are? Some people sadly don't have nearly as many choices as you do. Revel in your wonderful existence, and when you do this every day, appreciation and joy will appear throughout your life. Trust me, it's an incredible feeling.

"OK, hang on, Eric," I can hear critics saying. "So what are you saying? You mean don't *try* for anything and just be content with what you have?"

No! Not at all. Go for it. Do what you want! Be the very best you can be!

What I'm saying is this: if you build your life on a foundation of thankfulness and humility (also very important), your life will suddenly seem like one of the most beautiful spectacles ever created.

Share the Love

For years, there were times when I had a one-track mind. The blinders were on, and I was completely focused on being the very best comic I could be, eager to cross the finish line and raise my arms triumphantly in the air.

And I got there a few times over.

But when I got there, it was kinda lonely, and I felt kinda shallow. I realized that life is not meant to be lived so singularly focused.

As we travel onward, we are supposed to help the people who cannot help themselves. So many people need help along the way or to be reminded of the joy that exists in the world. Take someone by the hand and cross the finish line together.

This is what it means to be human. This is what it means to make sure someone else gets to enjoy the wonderful blessings of this all-too-quick life.

Throughout my life, I've enjoyed doing something every day to make someone else happy. Sometimes I buy a sandwich for a homeless person and really look them in the eye to show I care. Other times it's making a CVS clerk laugh, deadpanning that I didn't like her "questionable service." (I really did. We'd both crack up.)

Yes, life is meant to be *shared*, so find a way to share your blessings with others. Help them discover the wonderful treasure inside themselves. There are many people that need you out there. Don't be afraid of how amazing you are.

So that is the list: trust yourself, choose joy (not happiness), and share the love.

Although I may have painted with a broad brush here, I firmly believe that if you follow these three suggestions, you will be so much better off in a life that often moves way too quickly.

And remember what I mentioned in the previous chapter: there are millions of people who have experienced exactly what you have and who have felt just as you do. But you know what?

This is your time.

I love you, I'm proud of you, I believe in you, and I'm here for you.

Now, can you do *one* last thing for me, before we move on? Just smile. You are exactly where you need to be. Now, get on out there, and make it a rewarding life.

SUNDAY SERMONS

I now want to stop sounding like a know-it-all (remember how much they bug me?) and take a moment to give all the glory and thanks to God, who not only inspires me to formulate my thoughts but gives me the courage to pass them on to others.

For the last few years, I have tried to inspire others with the same amazing love and direction that God has shown me in my humble existence by writing brief meditations every Sunday to post on Facebook.

What follows are a few of these "Sunday Sermons," and I hope they resonate with you.

Sunday Sermon: With a lot of headlines, events, and a new day upon us, this is a great time for personal reflection. Are you overwhelmed or in a good place? Confident? Feeling uncertain about something? Always know that the world will always keep doing what it is doing, so be a little selfish for your soul and take some time to sit with yourself. Listen to your heart and reestablish your relationship with God. Start with faith—faith that God has a plan for you; faith to not live in fear, but with hope and joy in your heart; faith that God has brought you this far AND THAT HE WOULD NEVER EVEN THINK OF STOPPING NOW. So keep trusting and putting in the effort. Things will be just fine . . . I promise you. Make it a great week!

Sunday Sermon: Dream big today. Pick something that moves you—a thought, a cause, a goal, a trepidation—and just follow through, for it is not about the result. It is about faith and lessons learned and trusting the relationship between you and God! His love is there—it's ALWAYS there—and the wonderful outcome awaits you. Rejoice, and make it a great week!

Sunday Sermon: Someone is hoping you will reach out to them today. Perhaps they could use some encouragement. Surprise them, and show them the same love that God continually gives you. A special rekindling awaits you. Make it a great week!

Sunday Sermon: Keep the faith in times of trouble. When you are at your breaking point and want to quit, go a few feet more. God wants you to be a little uncomfortable, or you might not have moved. While moving toward your destiny and unique blessings, make it a great week!

Sunday Sermon: Your strength is more powerful than you know. You are here today, aren't you? All the things in the past that you thought were doom and gloom, you got through with flying colors. Keep that attitude today and always. Count on yourself. Good things will happen, and always remember where that strength comes from—a loving God who blesses you every day. "All things are possible through Christ who strengthens me" was written for a reason. Make it a great week!

Sunday Sermon: Why are your troubles and failures self-magnified, but your accomplishments are taken for granted? Why do we focus on what is "wrong" and ignore all that is going "right"? The truth is, it is all going as planned, so give yourself some credit today and be thankful. And if things get hard this week, give your heart a break! You are doing great! Your faith will be, and is being, rewarded not as some sort of bargaining game, but as a wonderful molding of righteousness, strength, and character for the long term. So get excited, and make it a great week!

Sunday Sermon: In this complex world, it's nice to take a step back and focus on the basics. Every day is always an opportunity to cherish family, friendships, laughs, traditions, and other reminders that tell us how lucky we are—lucky to be growing, changing, and evolving—while still holding on to the little things, WHICH ARE REALLY THE BIG THINGS. Don't forget to treat every day with that same joy and appreciation, for it is contagious, and your power can change others for the better. Make it a great week!

Sunday Sermon (from the road): Have you ever really thought how many chances we get from God? In work, hobbies, forgiveness, and relationships, this is all possible because God gave up his only Son to die for our sins. In this day and age, I understand that social media may not be the place for these kind of specifics, but we have been told "if anyone is ashamed of me and my words, the Son of man will be ashamed of them." So be proud of who you are and what you believe in, and be thankful for what are two of the greatest gifts—mercy and grace. Make it a great week!

Sunday Sermon: Whether we are excited about something that seems to take forever to get here or are very frustrated with something that seems to chip away at us, both of these emotions require a very important trait: PATIENCE. Please know that with hard work, it will pay off, and times that seem to drag on uncomfortably—they will pass. Nothing lasts forever, not the good or the bad, so take joy in the process, and just do your best—because it is GOOD ENOUGH. God is watching over you, and He knows that the test leads to the TESTament. Have patience, stay faithful, and be joyous. Make it a great week!

Sunday Sermon: As you reflect back upon the day, be proud of yourself and realize how blessed you are, even in a landscape that is not always just or fair. Keep going, keep praying, and keep being joyful! There are two roads, one of adventure and one of regret. Choose the adventure, and go for it! Feel the love from above. Make it a great week!

Sunday Sermon: God's love is like a heavenly car wax—a special, impenetrable coverage of love that will ensure all the tears, pain, frustrations, and disappointments just ROLL OFF YOU. Deep down, you'll know that you will always be just fine, so don't ever doubt that. That's right. Faith plus God's love? Quite an incredible combination! Make it a great week!

Sunday Sermon: As you reflect on the year, remember that despite the tears, pain, and frustrations, you are still here! Right now! And you're a better person for it! I challenge you now to continue this journey and go into the new year with three fundamental things—forgiveness, *passion, and effort. That's right. First, make sure you forgive yourself and others to create a clean slate. Get back to loving yourself and others, then keep discovering what you do best with passion and effort. Do not worry about the results, as I ask you to just let life happen. Keep making those necessary adjustments, but keep loving consistently with joy in your heart, as we get to see another year on this earth yet have "one less" year to our existence. So make it count. And when things get too much to handle, you know exactly where to go—to a loving God that simply, unequivocally, without a doubt ADORES YOU! So don't think too much. Just keep smiling, and always remember—every single day—you are exactly where you need to be!*

Make it a great YEAR!

Well, I think you get the picture.

I'm not a preacher or trying to be, but I'm someone who really, really cares—not just about my journey, but yours as well.

And when you keep what I mentioned above in the forefront of your mind, I really do believe that you'll have a much more enjoyable and trusting existence, not only on this earth but in preparation *for the next life to come.*

Thanks for reading, and may God bless you.

CHILLS AND THRILLS!

And because I firmly believe in God and a heaven, I also believe in the paranormal. I don't want to get into all the reasons why (although I am extremely passionate about this subject, so don't tempt me), but I do want to tell you about one fall evening on the road, when I had one of the most thrilling and terrifying experiences of my life.

When you do a college, you are a guest in a new town and must acclimate to the area—the people, the culture, the food—the history.

In all my twenty-seven years of traveling to nearly every nook and cranny of the United States, I never was so enamored and caught up in what a town offered than the Civil War paranormal experience of Gettysburg, Pennsylvania.

The moment you arrive, you realize that this town is unlike anything you have ever experienced before. We're not just talking about one or two statues across the street from a nail salon and a McDonald's. No, this was the real deal. Statues and monuments everywhere! After just one hour of walking around, you forget what year it is, as if you've been sent back to 1861. You won't see a single modern chain anything anywhere.

Instead, you walk on the original dirt roads and encounter people dressed in period clothes, lanterns illuminating old houses, and dozens of landmarks. There is even a spot fabled to be where Lincoln wiped his brow before giving the famous Gettysburg Address! The whole town is incredible.

Wanting to fully embrace the moment and pacify my paranormal prowess at the same time, I decided to stay, according to an official poll, at the sixth most haunted hotel in the United States. And I use the word "hotel" very loosely because, in fact, it was an old, tiny house with *the original bullet holes* created by Southern soldiers trying to shoot former slaves hiding up in the attic. And if that's not enough, when you enter the side of the house and walk up the old, creaky wooden stairs to one of only three bedrooms, you realize that unless you decide to read an old, dusty book from one of the cobwebbed bookshelves, it is going to be a very long and eerie night.

How eerie? Let's just say that as soon as I got to my antique bedroom, the grumpy owner of the house called my room to tell me that not only was I the only one staying over, but there was, and I quote, "no refund if you decide to leave in the middle of the night because I just had a spooked couple take off at 3:00 a.m., and they wanted their money back."

In my best excited yet nervous voice, I said, "No problem."

Seeing the darkness approaching, I knew that I had to fully engage myself in haunted Gettysburg before turning in for what was sure to be an eventful night. So I drove out to one of the major paranormal hot spots in town—the actual Civil War battlefield where tens of thousands of soldiers died. Driving my rental car down the dusty dirt road, now in the dead of night, I nervously checked my rearview mirror, only seeing the trail of gravel smoke visible by the red taillights, and finally found a place to park. With the windows down, the engine turned off, and the headlights on, the only thing I heard were the crickets chirping in the background. Other than that, it was dead quiet.

But I wasn't done yet.

For in order to fully engage in the haunted experience, I realized I needed to turn off my headlights, call upon any fallen soldier to reveal himself, and patiently wait for a response, completely vulnerable in the blackest of night.

So I did. One minute went by. Nothing. Another minute went by. Nothing again.

Maybe I need to *demand* that a soldier stand in front of my car and reveal himself?

So I did. I commanded it! I told all the soldiers that I was about to blast on my headlights and that I wanted to see someone in full uniform with rifle standing in front of the car. Whoever came, so be it!

And as I reached for the headlight crank, I counted to three. One, two, and I blasted the lights on!

I didn't see or hear a thing. (Well, other than what might have been liquid running down my leg. What the hell was I thinking?!)

I turned the car on, spun the tires, and got the hell out of there.

Back at the hotel, where I was certain a pissed-off soldier was probably waiting for me, I am now alone.

There is no one else staying there in the other two bedrooms. There was no TV, no radio, and of course, no Wi-Fi. Though still a bit unnerved, I quickly became bored. So what did I do next?

Hmm, why not take a tour of the house by myself?

(I know. Don't ask.)

For the next hour and a half, I walked around every creaky floor, hallway, and cubby hole that this sixth most haunted hotel had to offer, literally ducking my head as I entered every room. (Why everyone was so small back in the day, I have no idea.)

And then I heard it. And it was loud.

One of the other locked bedroom doors began violently rattling back and forth. There house was so old that there was a little give in the door frame, but this shaking was far beyond natural. The round metal doorknob was going berserk.

All I could think of was the frightening Google review that I had remembered from earlier—that a small child, who was trampled by a horse in the front yard, was carried up to one of the bedrooms, where he died in agony. Yet, even in death, he was so "playful" and "mischievous if woken up"—probably just another term for pissed off— that he would forcefully yank on your bed covers at night while you slept!

Oh, and if you didn't wake up quickly enough? He would then do the honor of throwing loose change off your nightstand.

"Welp. See ya! Time to go!" I mumbled.

And of course, lucky me, I then turn to reopen what I thought was my bedroom door and inadvertently open up the *attic* door—where, again, the dozens of slaves who were hiding from the South, and who survived being shot at, had died from disease and malnutrition.

Ah yes, how lovely.

So after racing down the dimly lit hallway to the correct door to grab my overnight bag (I was already bravely wearing my coat and hat and had never unpacked), I then decided to waste even more time running from this ghost child and bent over the bathroom sink to splash some cold water on my face. (And of course, I was absolutely terrified and just prayed that one of the angry battlefield soldiers wouldn't appear in the mirror.)

I paused and lifted my head up. Nope. No soldier. No annoyed ghost child.

OK, *now* we can get the hell out of here?

After racing down those side stairs like a madman, I ran out the door. I was never so glad to see my rental car and was so thankful it wasn't some horse and carriage. Hell, I needed speed at this point.

But then something odd happened.

Don't ask me how or why, but as I sat there safe in the running car, a wave of melancholy come over me.

And like a ton of bricks, it suddenly hit me. My haunted adventure was now over.

My anxiety, which had turned to calm, had now just turned into a feeling of being extremely bummed out.

Geez, what was I so afraid of? I thought. Should I go back upstairs? I mean, the room is paid for. And who knows, maybe it wasn't the ghost child? And even if it was, c'mon, Eric. It's just a little kid! Hell, maybe we can both throw some change off the nightstand and make a game of it!

(*Fast-forward.*)

I was never so happy to be thirty miles away in a Hampton Inn next to a twenty-four-hour Denny's, where the bad, mean ghosts couldn't get me anymore.

UFO-HELL NO!

And on that note, let's talk about UFOs and extraterrestrials. They're not only coming. They're already here. And they've been here for a very, very long time.

Yeah, that's right. I said it. And for those of you who don't believe, what the heck are you thinking? I mean—how on *earth* could you not?

OK, no more joking around.

When it comes to UFOs and their existence, I find it incredibly frustrating, close minded, and almost arrogant to think that we are the only things that exist in the universe. Have you ever seen the models estimating the immense size of what we are actually talking about here? We are such tiny specks of specks of specks in this universe, it's hard to fathom the scale we're talking about here. I lost track of our *galaxy* the last time I looked at one of these models.

It was incredible!

There was Earth, then our solar system, then our galaxy, then the Milky Way. But then the Milky Way is put in the context of other freakin' galaxies with solar systems and their own collections of planets!

And still, that's just a subset of the entire cosmos!

We're actually running out of letters and numbers to give temporary names to all of these worlds!

So please don't tell me that there is nothing else out there.

OK, I hear the skeptics argue, "Well, fine. So there are thousands upon thousands of planets out there, but I'm sorry, *we* are the only life-forms that exist."

Really? After running those numbers, *that* is your answer? Don't ever go to a casino and play the odds, 'cause you'll lose your shirt.

And then the skeptics start to panic. "Well, what *proof* do you have that they exist?"

Hmm, let's see. Only dozens upon dozens of clear videos and incidents seen by thousands of people at the same time—even ones confirmed by just about every government in the world!

That's right. Even the highest-ranking officials in every country are now spilling the beans. Why? Because there is too much video and audio proof that has come to light. And no, not videos by some "hick farmer" who ran out with his shotgun in the middle of the night because the horses got spooked. These sightings regularly happen with our very own top-ranked military pilots and staff, and many are admitting exactly what they saw.

Look, it was just a matter of time.

Now I'll admit I don't know why extraterrestrials are here or when they first arrived, but we do know from looking at the ancient drawings in caves and even inside the Egyptian pyramids that there are *clear* illustrations of UFOs from ancient times.

(And no, skeptics, that is not a carving of a giant platter with spaghetti shooting down from the sky. It's the real deal. Look it up.)

So now we have video, military evidence, and historical evidence of other life visiting our planet—just a grain of sand on the proverbial beach of the universe.

Are you still not convinced?

I understand. It's certainly easier to accept that our little planet—with our little stock market, sports teams, reality shows, and "high-tech" social media—is the only thing that exists and that we are, and always have been, the *only* intelligent life that has ever existed.

Fine, I respect that (well, not really).

Try this analogy.

Picture the universe as a gigantic New York City apartment building. The earth is your little apartment, and it has all your belongings inside. But then imagine that, due to financial and technological limitations, you cannot leave the apartment. Yes, you can open the door and peek outside every now and again. You can see some of the other doors on your floor—Mars, Venus, the moon. How nice. But again, while you may still be aware of the *hundreds* of other floors in this skyscraper, being stuck in your room means you have not had the chance to see them for yourself.

But they are there. They do exist. We know this.

Are you now telling me that every other apartment in the building is vacant? Or that no one with better capabilities has *ever* come to your floor, touched your door, or even peeked underneath it?

Would you say this just because you haven't seen it for yourself?

Hmm . . . or maybe you at least recognize the possibility but for some reason—maybe ego, fear, or just plain stubbornness—still just don't want to believe it.

That's OK. As a roommate coexisting with you in this Earth-apartment, I still love ya—so much so that I'll even do the dishes tonight.

But I guarantee that we *will* be talking about this again later!

As with everything, it's only a matter of time.

TOUCHED BY AN ANGEL

OK, now that I've gotten you in the mindset of the afterlife and the unexplainable, I want to tell you about an occurrence that still makes me scratch my head to this day. I am telling you this not to defend my beliefs in the previous two chapters, nor am I trying to convince you of anything.

I simply have a story to tell and can hardly believe.

The place was a Staten Island train station in the fall of 2012.

I had just gotten off a crazy run of college shows and was off to headline the Tropicana in Atlantic City. I was exhausted. But I still managed to pack a bag and take a ferry to the Amtrak holding area, where I would wait patiently for my train. The place was just about empty, and I got there early (which was good because I had extra time to mentally switch gears to my club set from my college one.) But again, I was tired, stressed, and hunched over on a bench after a long stretch on the road.

And it showed on my face.

But as I lifted my head up, there was a man—a man unlike anyone or anything I had ever seen before. He was an older, husky gentleman full of life, perhaps like someone's peppy grandfather with lots of stories to tell. But what was so unique was the fact that he was dressed in a pristine white three-piece suit, white top hat, and white cane. He looked like a shiny new penny, and he definitely didn't belong in this era, never mind a quiet train station at three o'clock in the afternoon.

He also had no bags, which I found odd. He was just sitting there smiling at me. And it wasn't creepy whatsoever. It was a comforting smile with a purpose, almost like he knew something that I didn't and needed to tell me.

He did. And I'll never forget it.

In an empty terminal, this angelic, peacefully smiling man confidently said to me, "Don't worry so much. You look like a very special man with very special gifts."

I didn't know what to say back other than thank you. Needing something to drink and realizing that I had to get out of my head for a moment, I got up to go to the vending machine. It might have only taken thirty seconds.

But as I turned around to take the short walk back to my seat, the mystery man was gone. He'd vanished without a trace. I nervously looked all around the empty terminal for him. There was no sign of him, but more importantly, there was no way he could have made it to the exit in that time.

What in the hell just happened? I pondered. Is this a joke? Am I imagining things?

I sat back down next to my bag and kept swiveling my head around to see whether he'd would come back. He never did. So as I boarded the train and made it through a spectacular weekend of shows, it was not until the train ride back that I had a moment to try to make sense of this unexplainable experience I had.

Who. Was. This. Man? Why was he dressed like that? Why was he sitting there alone with no luggage? Why did he talk to me with such comforting words?

How did he know I *needed* such comforting words?

I can't explain what happened nor will I try to. I am simply going to tell you that this is the God's honest truth, and I don't make stuff up like this for attention. I take the afterlife very seriously and believe that this man was sent to me for a reason that I will never fully understand, but am so appreciative of.

But if I had to say, I think God knew I needed some help—some confidence and some assurance that everything was going to be all right—and sent one of his angels to relay this heartfelt message to me.

I'll say it again. I am not here to try to convince you of anything.

And I'll leave that right here.

I know what I saw. I know what I believed then. And I know what I still believe to this day.

This was something out-of-this-world spectacular that can't be explained.

And for those who still doubt me, wondering how I could believe that this was a sign from above, that's OK.

Actually, thank you.

You just reinforced what faith is.

DR. E., RELATIONSHIP COUNSELOR

I know what you're thinking. Why would I ever take advice from a guy who has never been married or had kids? Well, the answer is simple. Although I am no relationship expert—nor am I trying to be one—I have learned some very important relationship lessons that I can share with you, despite being single.

Hopefully what I share can help you navigate your various friendships and romances, and create much more fulfilling, mutual bonds that last a lifetime.

Getting right to it, here are some guidelines that I have discovered through both disappointing and joyous moments that have made me a better man.

Never Settle . . . But Don't Be Too Picky

Don't ever settle.

You hear this phrase all the time, but what does it actually mean? At first glance, it probably seems closely related to never compromising who you are.

And that's perfectly true. Sure, if there's someone you have nothing in common with and whose values you are simply not attracted to, it's more than OK to wish them well and walk away.

But now, let's expand on this notion.

You also have to remember that no one is perfect.

So when it comes to the smaller issues—the things that are maybe not a part of the wonderful chemistry you have—please keep an open mind. Most times, you'll be better off if you're flexible and recognize someone's "faults" as opportunities for the two of you to grow. And if you do so with humor and honesty, learning to work as a team in this way makes you both much more vulnerable.

It took a long time for me to accept that we are all flawed. We all want that perfect person. But I'll tell you right now: such a person doesn't exist! Trust me, by dismissing a terrific person who is 95 percent perfect for you, you're missing out on someone truly special.

And from personal experience, I can tell you that this is no way to live your life. (Honestly, I can tell you right now, that I do *not* want someone exactly like me! Hell, I shiver at imagining two frugal-minded, grumpy, minimalist, napping addicts who do the same introverted things over and over. Seriously, we'd never leave the house!)

In short, you can't expect someone to be a perfect match. But if 95 percent of the physical attraction, mental attraction, values, and respect is there, jump on it—well, figuratively speaking (OK, and literally).

Don't Play with Anyone's Heart

In a nutshell, doing this is just wrong. And I've been on both sides of this issue as a younger man—no, definitely not deliberately, and thankfully not often—but when you are twenty-five and have raging hormones, an ego, and a naive shortsightedness, you might accidentally go after what you want without thinking of the repercussions. Specifically then, our selfishness can not only hurt someone's feelings in the short term, but perhaps derail their destiny and happiness in the long run.

And that is not good. Not in the slightest.

So be aware of how you feel about someone and how they feel about you. Sometimes the brave thing—and the right thing—is to let go of someone so they can find their soul mate. This honors both their existence and the very short time we all have on this earth.

Pay attention and do the right thing.

Don't Try to Save the Unsavable

Now, the first thing you might notice here is the word "unsavable." Immediately you might want to say that *everyone* is savable. True, they are—but only if they want to save themselves. I've seen relationship after relationship (even my own) where one person is doing all the damage, and the other person is stuck cleaning up the mess. Although no one is perfect, always remember that no one—*no one*—has the right to take advantage of you and drag you down with them!

If your partner is hung up on drugs, alcohol, infidelity, gambling, abuse, a bad temper, passive-aggressive games—whatever—your health and happiness should never take a back seat!

And I've heard all the excuses before in trying to justify staying together: "Well, I'm going to give them one more chance" or the ever-popular "But I love them!"

I'm sure you do love them, but you need to love yourself first and get out of the relationship. And I know that sounds harsh. I've even heard people follow up with "But I just can't get up and leave! They would *die* without me. I can't abandon them now!"

No. But you can walk away and let a professional deal with that problem, which *most likely existed before you even got there* and almost certainly has *nothing to do with you*!

Think of it this way. Picture yourself standing on the edge of a cliff. Your troubled partner is dangling off the edge—just pleading for you to help them up, apologizing over and over, and crying out, "Please, save me! I'll never do it again!" Then the minute you begin to pull them up—after sweating and grunting and expending so much mental and physical energy—they go right back to their unhealthy behaviors.

Why would anyone stay in a relationship like that?

Why would *you* stay in a relationship like that?

You deserve better.

And that's why, when you find your partner dangling off that edge, pleading with you over and over to save them, you simply say, "I love you, but I can't do that anymore. I *won't* do that anymore." And before you go, you look behind you and try to find a much stronger hand—preferably a professional's hand—to take over from there and do the heavy lifting.

But there is more. Much more.

After you do that, you then need to take the even more important step and ask yourself *why* and *how* you found yourself in that situation. And make no mistake, it will take 100 percent of your courage and honesty to really dig deep—perhaps deeper than you ever have before—and find the truth.

Why did you stay with that person?

Maybe you didn't think you could do better. Maybe you didn't want to be alone. Maybe you had some good times that took the attention off the toxic ones. Maybe it was the great sex. Maybe your *self-esteem* wasn't where it needed to be.

So you put up with it, and you stayed.

But deep down, you knew something was wrong—and you just knew that you deserved better.

As for me, I have never personally been in a relationship truly that toxic, but I sure have done some second-guessing and wondered about the happier existence out there for me.

And now, heeding my own advice, I'm on a more exciting and fulfilling path.

Because in the end, the goal should be to search with some honest effort for a real, healthy, long-lasting, rewarding relationship—which is the way a relationship is truly meant to be.

Find Yourself to Find Someone Else

Ah, finally, the great quest of trying to find that special someone to share your life with! While this can be exciting, fast-paced, and I-just-wanna-give-up-and-hide-between-the-mattresses frustrating all at once, here's one thing you should *never* do when selecting a mate: focus extra attention on your significant other to hide from yourself.

Allow me to explain by being open about my own past struggles.

We all have fears and insecurities that cause us to second-guess and not be fully present as our true selves. And as I look back on a few of my relationships, I see that I often unconsciously chose mates waging some internal battles. By choosing these wonderful yet unhealthy people, I was able to focus my energy on "fixing" them while allowing myself to hide from my own insecurities and struggles.

With the spotlight placed on the other person—to help, to fix, to support—I not only gave myself a free pass on working on myself, but also (and check this out) created the opportunity to become her hero in the process! That's right. I was the knight in shining armor who swooped in to save the day!

To be honest, it's great to feel that kind of love from your mate, but when you don't fully value yourself, that adoration is never going to be fully savored. In turn, the love, although sincere, then only becomes a temporary, feel-good distraction from doing the hard work you need to do on yourself—the hard work that involves honesty, vulnerability, and character.

At the end of the day, a strong relationship is about two healthy people trying to make their lives work *together*, not about an unhealthy give-and-take facade riddled with fear and overcompensation.

So before jumping into a relationship, really get honest with yourself, and get to know yourself first. Then choose a mate who is ready to make you a better person, and vice versa. Together you can then build a partnership built on mutual transparency, effort, respect, and healthy self-esteem.

I promise you, when that is achieved, the two of you will be pretty damn indestructible!

And I'm gonna leave that right there.

Thank you for coming in today. Oh, and there's no charge for this session.

But if you'd quickly exit this page to your right, that would be great. I've got a two o'clock coming in very shortly to discuss her obsession with screaming at paper clips.

Sigh.

Wish me luck.

MY MANY LOVE AFFAIRS!

No, sorry to disappoint you, but we aren't talking about *those* love affairs here. And although it would've been cool to make up some erotic story that I spent a hot weekend in Barbados with Adriana Lima—seriously, who would I be kidding?

(And I wouldn't have blamed you for not believing me.)

Instead, let's just stick with some nerdy facts about my other love affairs—that is, some of the other wonderful things that really move me as a person. (Again, I'm excited to do this just to see what we have in common and to perhaps spark some new, interesting thoughts in your mind.)

So, here we go in no particular order.

I love how a positive attitude is the blueprint for my life. I love how I, and only I, am responsible for my life. I love how I have a daily choice to be either miserable, or rise up, and be joyful. I love how I realize that, although wonderful, holidays, parties, and "downtime" won't get me to where I want to go. I love how I must put in the work. I love how it is not always easy. I love how new discoveries become that much sweeter. I love passing on those new discoveries to someone else.

I love the fact that I get to do what I love for a living and still be there for my family. I love the fact that I get to repay my mom back for all the sacrifices and hard work she showed us by making sure she is well cared for in her golden years. I love that fact that there isn't a day that goes by that I don't think of my grandfather, who taught me to drive, shave, and work hard with character. I love the fact that I get to dote on my brother's and sister's kids, and pass on so many of the life lessons and family traditions that I have been so blessed with—which keeps that wheel of love movin'.

I love that I try, to the best of my ability, to live a Christlike life and push myself to be both strong and selfless, even when it isn't easy. I love the fact that I have made so many great friends along the way during my life's journey. I love the fact that I might have just changed someone's life for the better—even if just for a minute—through my comedy.

I love that fact that I am able to forgive.

I love the fact that people have forgiven me.

I love looking back at how hard I fell at times but was still able to get back up, changing not only the current situation, but also filing away an important lesson for reference. I love that I honor my past, recognize the present, and plan for the future.

I love my alone time to recharge. I love how sensitive I am.

I love that I was taught about finances and investing.

I love the fact that Gramps taught me about the "unforeseen factor"—that is, just when everything seems to fall into place and you are emotionally riding sky high, feeling indestructible, *always* be aware of that one thing that could destroy everything.

I love the fact, however, that I was never taught to live in fear.

I love the education I received. I love all the teachers, priests, and nuns who provided the best foundation a boy could ask for. I love that I still talk to all my friends and teachers to this day.

I love the fact that I am a minimalist. I love the fact that I don't need "things" to make me happy. I love my incredibly flat feet, even if they get a me a new hip pretty soon. I love being a creature of habit, yet I also love wandering off physically and mentally into unchartered waters.

I love all the animals, even the bees that have stung me.

I love my dandruff and dry scalp.

I love having air-conditioning. I love having heat. I love simply being able to flush a toilet and not having to dig a hole. I love being six feet tall (in shoes) and 185 pounds. I love my soft hands. I love my skinny wrists. I love knowing that I still need to take care of myself because I have a huge appetite with old age looming right around the corner.

I love waking up and being in control of my life while—yes, I know—still respecting the "unforeseen factor."

I love opening up my eyes every morning knowing that, with a little effort, I can not only change my life but the lives of so many others for the better.

I love that I am no longer as hesitant to embrace how very powerful I am as a human being.

I love the fact that you took the time to read my book.

I love the fact that, perhaps—just perhaps—we got to get a little bit closer.

Yep, if you haven't guessed yet . . . I love you.

CHEW ON THIS

Welp, I'm going to make this my final chapter of "content" because I've got some very disturbing news. This news is quite personal to me, yet it's something I am willing to share. It sometimes stops me in my tracks, making me worry about the future and long for the past. This news brings a tear to my eye when I think about facing this unavoidable truth: I am dying.

But please don't feel sorry for me.

Because so are you. (I bet that makes you feel better!)

You see, every moment that goes by is another step forward toward becoming no longer of this world. And guess what? This world *will* continue to go on without you, celebrating, eating, laughing, screwing, driving, working, protesting, fighting, spending, bragging, attending, and then celebrating again.

Now, I don't say this to sound depressing or negative. Quite the contrary!

Truth is, you were born at a specific point in history—not in prehistoric times, Roman times, or the eighteenth century. Now. This is where you are, in this particular era, with its own cultures, peoples, inventions, and world affairs.

And yes, there were millions of people who lived before you who didn't have it as good, and there will be millions more later on who will simply laugh at your naïve efforts to live the good life.

But right now, this is your chance to live a life—*your life.*

How are you going to spend it?

Unfortunately, ego and insecurity smugly answer, "I don't know" or "I'll think about that later because of XYZ."

Ahh, yes. The "because." Because something else is "more important," or because we are too busy or too afraid. We give in to the routine and, unfortunately, don't think of life in terms of wonderful, singular, precious moments.

Instead, we look at calendars, appointments, holiday seasons, months, and years. Then, when you add in being "distracted" by your responsibilities, family, work, ego, and fear (there are those two words again), you wake up wondering where the time has gone.

Now, I am not implying that your life is not fulfilling or that you are unhappy. If you're satisfied with where you are, terrific. Don't change a thing. But if there is even an ounce of regret, a sliver of frustration, a lingering yearning, please stop what you're doing this instant, and take stock of yourself—today.

Look in the mirror and ask yourself, "What is it that I want? What do I deserve from others? What impact do I want to leave on this world?"

Well, here's an idea. How about start by telling someone that you love them, or maybe throw caution to the wind and just do that thing that literally scares the shit out of you.

Whatever it is, just *do* something! And do it with character, passion, and effort.

Character, because it simply provides the most rewarding way to live. Don't cheat yourself or others. Do it the *right* way. (And you know when you're not, so knock it off!)

Passion, because it draws up every ounce of your being and doesn't allow time for self-doubt. (Stop with the crappy excuses and just go for it!)

Effort, because although it may not come easily, effort is what makes each moment, each step, each victory, a big one, so celebrate it. (And I ask that you savor the process!)

Yes, you owe yourself this.

So I am pleading with you. Please, *please* don't let your existence just become a series of statistics. Don't just be what the world thinks success is with its vanilla, shallow, structured purpose for you.

I am asking you to simply live *by doing what makes you feel alive.*

Don't waste another day.

The clock is ticking—right now, even as you're reading this.

Go find your true self.

Be honest as you drive toward your purpose.

And please know—heck, *always* know—that I'm undoubtedly your biggest fan.

Thank you for spending this time with me. I couldn't have done it without you.

SO LONG, BUT NEVER GOODBYE

And on that note, I don't have too much more to say.

I've discussed a lot, and I'm sure I will kick myself for forgetting a few things. But for now, I hope you not only enjoyed spending this time together but also got something out of it, something to take with you—something that *inspired* you.

And now, for the big reveal.

What was the meaning of the title? What did I mean by "richest comedian"?

Was I making a financial statement? Was it arrogance? Well, I think you already figured it out by now, but in case you didn't, I hope this clears it up.

On a chilly night in Arizona, at the rawest open mic night in the middle of a Mexican restaurant, were four comics waiting to practice five minutes of material to a crowd of zero.

And it was my turn.

Walking by the empty tables, I got introduced on stage as "the richest comedian you never heard of."

Although I knew that this nice person was just paying me a compliment and giving me a hard time about financial gains of such a difficult career path, I just smiled and clung to that *other* definition of "rich."

That genuine feeling of being completely, abundantly *fulfilled*—by finishing a journey, by embracing lessons learned, by overcoming the odds, by being at the right place at the right time.

The result? Pure *contentment*... far surpassing anything that I could have ever asked for.

Yes, God is indeed great.

So thank you for reading, and thank you to all who have blessed me along the way.

My hope now, as you leave here, is that you inspire someone—anyone—to take your love and passion and turn it into something greater for themselves.

With an unlimited abundance of love, light, and joy,

Eric

MY LIFE IN PICTURES

(See? I wasn't making this stuff up.)

MY FIRST CHRISTMAS

GRAMPS

YOUNG ERIC

THE RICHEST COMEDIAN YOU'VE NEVER HEARD OF

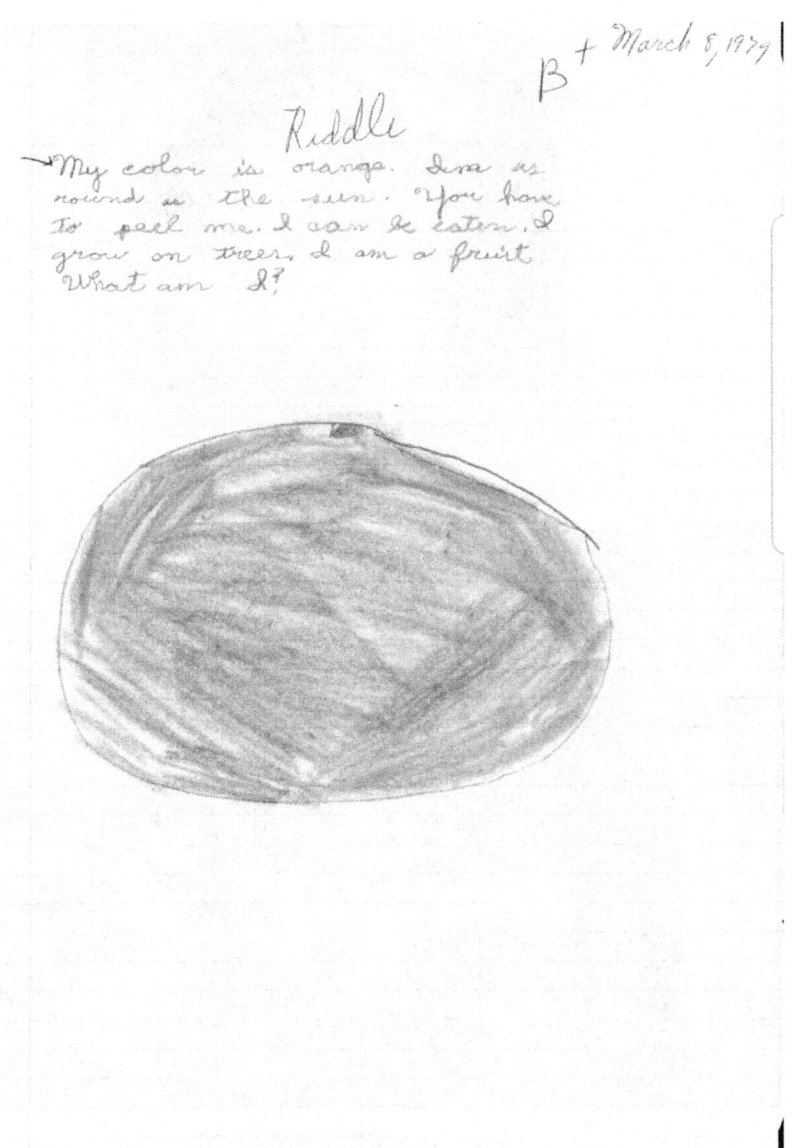

MY FIRST JOKE

ALL OF US

FAME AND FORTUNE

THE RICHEST COMEDIAN YOU'VE NEVER HEARD OF

Milwaukee's Very Own Safe House

4th Annual Comedy Competition

& American Cancer Society Benefit

Date; Sept. 16, 1993
Time; 8:30 PM
Place; Safe House

Class A & B Competition

271-2007 Reservations Requested for parties of 4 or more

764-6790 Dan Manke M.C. To Apply For Stage Time

International Exports, Ltd.
779 NORTH FRONT STREET • MILWAUKEE, WISCONSIN 53202
PHONE: (414) 271-2007

MY COMEDY DEBUT

THE BAD BOY OF FIGURE SKATING

MY WEST 78TH AND BROADWAY APARTMENT

THE RICHEST COMEDIAN YOU'VE NEVER HEARD OF

MIKE MYERS

PHIL HARTMAN

THE RICHEST COMEDIAN YOU'VE NEVER HEARD OF

MY BOY BAND DAYS

MUCH BETTER!

HANDPICKED EXTRA (BY ARROW)
FOR THE MOVIE MAJOR LEAGUE

THE RICHEST COMEDIAN YOU'VE NEVER HEARD OF

March 1, 1997

To whom it may concern,

I am a Talent Manager with The Barry Katz Entertainment Group. We represent many talented actors in film and television.

I have known Eric O'Shea since July 1996. After presenting his act, to various high profile entertainment industry members, we received tremendous response and interest. Many of the industry executives were so impressed with his talents, creativity and hard work; they expressed interest in retaining him for a development deal. A process and dream most actors take years to achieve.

At present, Eric has signed with The Walt Disney Company for a development deal, which will earn Eric $125,000.00 in 1997. In the last month, SEM & M, one of the leading commercial agencies in New York, expressed interest in Eric. They are sending him out both as on-camera and as voice over talent. This has been an extremely lucrative field for many of our clients. I am confident that it will be a source of considerable income for Eric as well.

He is honest, respectful, has a strong work ethic and is admired by his peers both personally and professionally. It is a pleasure to work and represent such a talented, gifted actor and person.

Eric has my full endorsement and support.

Should you have any further questions, kindly contact the undersigned.

Maureen Taran
The Barry Katz Entertainment Group

MT/ko

MY HOLDING DEAL WITH DISNEY

Eric O'Shea

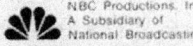

Standard AFTRA Engagement Contract
Network Television
Single Broadcast and Multiple Broadcast within One Calendar Week

NBC Productions, Inc.
A Subsidiary of
National Broadcasting Company, Inc.

Dated: 9/10/ 19 96
State of **CALIFORNIA**

Between ERIC O'SHEA
C/O BARRY KATZ MANAGEMENT
1776 BROADWAY
Suite 2001
NEW YORK, NY 10019

hereinafter called "Performer,"

and

NBC PRODUCTIONS, INC., A SUBSIDIARY OF NATIONAL BROADCASTING COMPANY hereinafter called "Producer"

Performer shall render artistic services in connection with the rehearsal and broadcast of the program(s) designated below and preparation in connection with the part or parts to be played.

TITLE OF PROGRAM: FRIDAY NIGHT
TYPE OF PROGRAM: Sustaining( ) Commercial(X) Closed Circuit( )
SPONSOR (if commercial): VARIOUS
NUMBER OF GUARANTEED DAYS OF EMPLOYMENT:
(if Par. 19 of the AFTRA Code is applicable)
PLACE OF PERFORMANCE*: NBC BURBANK
SCHEDULED FINAL PERFORMANCE DAY: 9/10/96
AFTRA CLASSIFICATION: SPECIALTY ACT OF 1
PART(S) TO BE PLAYED:
COMPENSATION: $832.00
MAXIMUM REHEARSAL HOURS INCLUDED IN ABOVE COMPENSATION:
(if Par. 56(b) of the AFTRA Code is applicable)

Execution of this agreement signifies acceptance by Producer and Performer of all of the above terms and conditions and those on the reverse hereof and attached hereto, if any.

Eric O'Shea
Performer

NBC PRODUCTIONS, INC.
A SUBSIDIARY OF
NATIONAL BROADCASTING COMPANY, INC.
By

Check to be made payable to ERIC O'SHEA
*Subject to change in accordance with AFTRA Code.

SCHEDULE OF COMPENSATION FOR REPLAYS (Not applicable to walk-ons and extras): ^AFTRA SCALE
*1st $ _____ *2nd $ _____ 3rd $ _____ 4th $ _____
5th $ _____ 6th $ _____ 7th and subsequent replays thereafter $ _____
(8th payment covers all succeeding re-plays. Overscale payments apply against re-play fees, as provided in Par. 18 hereof. If there is a commercial replay of a sustaining program the fee for that replay shall be increased by 25% if the minimum sustaining replay fee was specified above. See Par. 73(b) of AFTRA TV Network Code.)
*If this replay is over a national television network, add 20% of Performer's additional rehearsal and dubbing fees for the program.

SCHEDULE OF FOREIGN USE COMPENSATION (where required by Par. 73(f) B 1 (b) of AFTRA TV Network Code):
AREA 1 $ _____ AREA 2 $ _____ AREA 3 $ _____ AREA 4 $ _____
AREA 5 $ _____ (Areas are as defined in AFTRA TV Network Code)

NETWORK TELEVISION STANDARD TERMS AND CONDITIONS SEE ATTACHED RIDER

NBC FRIDAY NIGHT VIDEOS

THE RICHEST COMEDIAN YOU'VE NEVER HEARD OF

FLIRTING WITH THE CROWD AT NACA NATIONALS

FRESHMAN ORIENTATION TIME!

THE COUNTRY HAS SPOKEN

THE RICHEST COMEDIAN YOU'VE NEVER HEARD OF

THE CREATIVE EMMY AWARDS

CAROL BURNETT

SERIOUSLY, PINCH ME!

TV TIME

THE RICHEST COMEDIAN YOU'VE NEVER HEARD OF

WAVING TO THE CROWD AFTER A STANDING O

MY DRY BAR COMEDY SPECIAL

OPENING UP FOR SURVIVOR

THE RICHEST COMEDIAN YOU'VE NEVER HEARD OF

AWW . . . THEY LOVED ME

UNC'S GIRLS

MY NEPHEW AND BUDDY, EVAN

THE RICHEST COMEDIAN YOU'VE NEVER HEARD OF

DAVE WINFIELD

IN MY LUCKY GREEN HOODIE
AT YANKEE STADIUM FOR PLAYOFF GAME

JETER'S LAST GAME AT YANKEE STADIUM

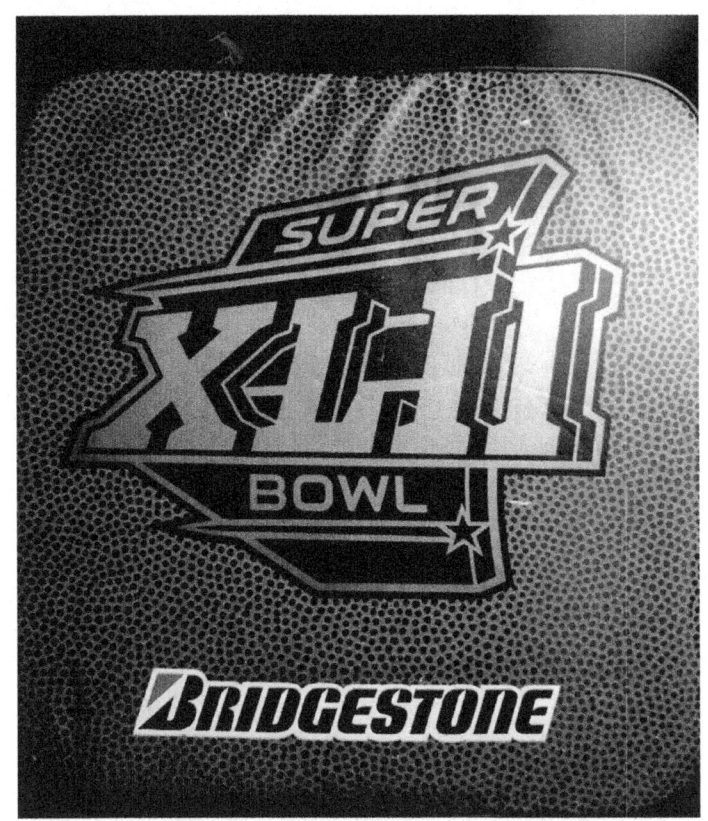

THE 2007 GIANTS' DAVID TYREE
HELMET CATCH SUPER BOWL

GASSIN' UP EMMY (M3)

THE MADONNA CONCERT

AND FINALLY . . . THE HOLY GRAIL
(THE FAMOUS MODEL PICTURE!)

Made in the USA
Monee, IL
06 December 2020